Christmas

Christmas
The Annual of Christmas Literature and Art

Volume Fifty-eight

Augsburg Publishing House
Minneapolis, Minnesota

In this volume

For most of us the celebration of the birth of Christ is encompassed in tradition. From the family gathered around the tree on Christmas Eve to hear the reading of the Christmas gospel to the presence of a favorite ethnic pastry, we celebrate with traditions. Some of those traditions have been developed within our families and are our own. "My 27-Cent Wise Man" chronicles the development of one family tradition centered on a child's creche.

In some communities the re-creation of customs that were a part of the celebration of our ancestors becomes a holiday tradition. The customs are no longer a part of our celebration, but the re-creation of them provides a sense of family. The article, "Pella Preserves Dutch Christmas," provides a glimpse into the celebration of an ethnic community.

Of course, there are some activities that are a part of the celebration of people of all nationalities. "Traditions in Common" highlights the singing of carols, the light motifs brought into our homes by the use of candles, the baking of cookies and pastries, the re-creation of the nativity scene, and the gathering of family members for a festive meal.

The composition of a new Christmas carol and the sharing of it with friends at Christmas has become a tradition for some people. The music displayed in this volume was originally written as Christmas greetings.

The successor to St. Nicholas, while not the focus of most of our celebrations, has become a traditional fixture of the season. "Nicholas: From Saint to Santa" outlines the evolution of one man's acts of generosity into a commercial enterprise.

What is traditional activity associated with the season for one generation is a memory for the next. The paintings by William Medcalf evoke memories of "Winter Activities of a Day Gone By."

And, for thousands of American families CHRISTMAS: The Annual of Christmas Literature and Art is also a part of their tradition. We hope that this volume becomes a part of your traditional celebration this year.

Table of Contents

Editorial staff: Leonard Flachman, Jennifer Huber; Richard Hillert, music consultant

4

The Christmas Story

According to St. Luke and St. Matthew

N ow in the sixth month the angel Gabriel was sent by God to a city of Galilee named Nazareth, to a virgin betrothed to a man whose name was Joseph, of the house of David. The virgin's name was Mary.

And having come in, the angel said to her, "Rejoice, highly favored one, the Lord is with you; blessed are you among women!"

But when she saw him, she was troubled at his saying, and considered what manner of greeting this was.

Then the angel said to her, "Do not be afraid, Mary, for you have found favor with God. And behold, you will conceive in your womb and bring forth a Son, and shall call his name Jesus. He will be great, and will be called the Son of the Highest; and the Lord God will give him the throne of his father David.

"And he will reign over the house of Jacob forever, and of his kingdom there will be no end."

Then Mary said to the angel, "How can this be, since I do not know a man?"

And the angel answered and said to her, "The Holy Spirit will come upon you, and the power of the Highest will overshadow you; therefore, also, that Holy One who is to be born will be called the Son of God."

And it came to pass in those days that a decree went out from Caesar Augustus that all the world should be registered. This census first took place while Quirinius was governing Syria. So all went to be registered, everyone to his own city.

And Joseph also went up from Galilee, out of the city of Nazareth, into Judea, to the city of David, which is called Bethlehem, because he was of the house and lineage of David, to be registered with Mary, his betrothed wife, who was with child.

So it was, that while they were there, the days were completed for her to be delivered.

And she brought forth her firstborn Son, and wrapped him in swaddling cloths, and laid him in a manger, because there was no room for them in the inn.

Now there were in the same country shepherds living out in the fields, keeping watch over their flock by night. And behold, an angel of the Lord stood before them, and the glory of the Lord shone around them, and they were greatly afraid.

Then the angel said to them, "Do not be afraid, for behold, I bring you good tidings of great joy which will be to all people. For there is born to you this day in the city of David a Savior, who is Christ the Lord. And this will be the sign to you: You will find a babe wrapped in swaddling cloths, lying in a manger."

And suddenly there was with the angel a multitude of the heavenly host praising God and saying:

"Glory to God in the highest, And on earth peace, good will toward men!"

So it was, when the angels had gone away from them into heaven, that the shepherds said to one another, "Let us now go to Bethlehem and see this thing that has come to pass, which the Lord has made known to us."

And they came with haste and found Mary and Joseph, and the babe lying in a manger. Now when they had seen him, they made widely known the saying which was told them concerning this child. And all those who heard it marveled at those things which were told them by the shepherds. But Mary kept all these things and pondered them in her heart. Then the shepherds returned, glorifying and praising God for all the things that they had heard and seen, as it was told them.

N ow after Jesus was born in Bethlehem of Judea in the days of Herod the king, behold, wise men from the East came to Jerusalem, saying, "Where is he who has been born King of the Jews? For we have seen his star in the East and have come to worship him."

When Herod the king heard these things, he was troubled, and all Jerusalem with him. And when he had gathered all the chief priests and scribes of the people together, he inquired of them where the Christ was to be born.

So they said to him, "In Bethlehem of Judea, for thus it is written by the prophet:

But you, Bethlehem, in the land of Judah,
Are not the least among the rulers of Judah;
For out of you shall come a Ruler
Who will shepherd my people Israel."

Then Herod, when he had secretly called the wise men, determined from them what time the star appeared. And he sent them to Bethlehem and said, "Go and search diligently for the young child, and when you have found him, bring back word to me, that I may come and worship him also."

When they heard the king, they departed; and behold, the star which they had seen in the East went before them, till it came and stood over where the young child was. When they saw the star, they rejoiced with exceedingly great joy.

And when they had come into the house, they saw the young child with Mary his mother, and fell down and worshiped him. And when they had opened their treasures, they presented gifts to him: gold, frankincense, and myrrh.

Then being divinely warned in a dream that they should not return to Herod, they departed for their own country another way.

Now when they had departed, behold, an angel of the Lord appeared to Joseph in a dream, saying, "Arise, take the young child and his mother, flee to Egypt, and stay there until I bring you word; for Herod will seek the young child to destroy him."

When he arose, he took the young child and his mother by night and departed for Egypt, and was there until the death of Herod, that it might be fulfilled which was spoken by the Lord through the prophet, saying, "Out of Egypt I called my Son."

A Silent Night
A Holy Night

WESLEY M. HARRIS

EVERY YEAR around the globe hearts and voices rise to the well-loved strains of "Silent Night." How did this beautiful carol come to be written? Well, it happened something like this. . . .

Snow propelled like clouds of nettles stung his face as Franz made his way through the drifts of snow that were piling up in the streets of Oberndorff. Icy blasts pummeled the town from the north. Franz had never felt so utterly cold. He shivered visibly and tightened his scarf against the raw winds of late December.

Passing by Kleinkopft's Bakery, he glanced through the gayly decorated windows to see Otto waving a cheery greeting from behind the tempting array of sweetbreads and pastries. Franz returned a half-hearted wave and a tired smile to his favorite pupil and thought, "How disappointed Otto will be when he learns the news. Confound those mice!"

It just didn't seem possible. Father Mohr had just informed Franz that the organ at the church was totally unusable. Mice had eaten their way through the bellows, making it leak so badly that hardly any air was forced through the organ pipes.

Last Sunday, Herr Grisinger (who had pumped the bellows on the organ for so many years) had told Franz, "It is getting more and more difficult to keep up the air pressure." But Franz had merely chalked it off as the result of Herr Grisinger's advancing years and the rheumatism that had plagued him for so long. But then Franz and Father Mohr had checked behind the organ console and Franz was forced to admit that the mice had done their job all too well. The organ simply could not be played until adequate repairs had been made.

Franz was tired—tired of teaching children, tired of correcting papers and tests, tired of choir rehearsals at church, tired of snow and cold, tired of the all-too-predictable behavior of the children as Christmas drew nearer and nearer. Even though it was the morning of Christmas Eve, he felt a weariness in his whole body as he plodded toward his flat over Pfieffer's Meat Market. Rounding the corner to the stairs, he drew a deep breath and felt the frigid rasp of the cold mountain air as it coursed through his lungs.

He coughed and hurried through the entryway, taking a moment to make sure the door was well secured against the winds, then made his way up the darkened steps to the landing outside his rooms. Even with the brightness of the snow piled high in the streets outside, his doorway seemed particularly dark and bleak as he lifted the latch to enter his lodgings. The fire in the grate was nearly gone; only a few glowing coals were left to drive the chill from his rooms. He hastened to add some kindling to the coals. On his hands and knees in front of the fireplace he blew gently through the embers so as to rekindle the fire. The muffler around his throat was too tight, so he took a moment to loosen it, then returned to coaxing the fire to burn more brightly.

It just didn't seem possible. Father Mohr had just informed Franz that the organ at the church was totally unusable. . . . Without the organ it was futile even to try to sing the mass.

Eventually a small flame flickered and began to grow, spreading through the bits of kindling that Franz had brought up from the woodpile the night before. As it began to take hold, he put on some larger pieces to sustain the heat a little longer. Then he straightened up, unwound the coils of muffler from around his neck, unbuttoned his greatcoat, removed his hat, and hung them on the rack by the door. Rubbing his hands together briskly, Franz thought again about the unhappy developments of the morning.

He recalled all too clearly that as far back as September he had mentioned to Father Mohr, "We really should write to Vienna and see if it might be possible to engage the services of an organ repairer before winter sets in." But Father Mohr had waited, hoping for approval by the vestry before allocating scarce funds from the church budget to be used for organ repair. That approval never came. So Franz had resigned himself to the fact that sections of the Rohrflöte and the Gemshorn would be out of tune for the Christmas mass. But he simply was not prepared for this. Now all of the choir's painstaking rehearsals of the Palestrina mass would be totally wasted. There would be no music for the Christmas Eve service.

Franz always did his work carefully, and the boys in the choir were as ready as they ever would be to sing the mass of the nativity. But without the organ it was futile even to try to sing the mass, for the lads simply could not carry the heavy musical burden without the instrument to lead them through the ancient harmonies. And with Oberndorff completely snowbound, there wasn't even a chance of getting the organ repairer through. Even worse, there had been no mail for almost two weeks, no word from his family and none of the mysterious packages that had always arrived just before Christmas. Franz had never felt quite so alone and forgotten as he did at that instant. As he pulled up a chair in front of the flickering flames on the hearth, he glanced around his bachelor billet and a sudden realization of how very poor he was swept over him.

"I could put up with all of this—the inadequate salary, the shabby clothes, even the isolation of Christmas away from the family—if only the organ might be made usable," he thought.

His mind wandered back to the summer day three years before when he had first made the trip to Oberndorff in the Tyrolean Alps at the request of the school trustees who wished to consider him for the position of schoolmaster for the tiny town. Franz had marveled, "What a beautiful little village! I would greatly enjoy teaching and living in such a place." As the coach slowly made its way over the rough roads leading to the town, he had craned his neck out of the window to catch the ever-changing vista of the Tyrol. When the coach finally drew to a stop in the town square, Franz had been very pleased with what he saw. But that had been in the beauty of summer, when the air was fresh with the scent of pine trees and mountain flowers.

Franz had tried to act reserved but amiable when he met with the burghers who served as the school trustees. Herr Kleinkopft, who arose to speak for the assembled burghers, had spoken very directly: "Herr Gruber, the appointment to this situation has a rather unusual requirement."

Franz had wondered, "Just what kind of a situation have I gotten myself into?"

Herr Kleinkopft explained the problem: "You see, Herr Gruber, the priest of our village church, Father Mohr, is a good man, an excellent preacher, and a real joy to our community. But, unfortunately, he cannot fill one duty that is usually a priest's responsibility. You see, Father Mohr has no ear for music and cannot possibly lead the choir of the church. Inasmuch as Father Mohr cannot fulfill this responsibility, it has been decided that the new schoolmaster must also be willing to assume the directorship of the choir in order to qualify for the position." Secretly, Franz couldn't have been more delighted, as his main delight at the university during his stu-

dent days had been singing with several different groups in the School of Music.

Franz had tried not to answer too quickly nor to seem too anxious, lest the good burghers feel he was a little *too* eager to receive the position. But he did manage to say, "I should be pleased to assume the directorship of the church choir in addition to my other responsibilities at the village school." As time passed, the boys choir showed such improvement the congregation and even the burghers were most complimentary to Franz over his work, both in the school and in the choir.

"I have written a few short verses. Perhaps you could put them to music, Herr Gruber."

Christmas this year had been a sort of goal for Franz. He had chosen the music for the Christmas Eve mass very carefully and had rehearsed it with the boys very thoroughly. Now, when all was in readiness, the organ would not play. Of course, the congregation could sing the familiar carols of Christmas without the organ. Father Mohr had been very specific about the singing of the well-known carols of Christmas, and Franz had agreed that the carols would present no problem, but what about the Palestrina mass? All the wonderful music that Franz and the boys had so carefully prepared would be lost.

Father Mohr had sighed and said, "Perhaps our congregation can just *say* the words of the mass until such time as when the organ can be repaired." Franz had risen to his feet and was reaching for his greatcoat in order to leave the rector's study when Father Mohr offered another suggestion: "Even though the organ is unusable, it would still be nice if the boys could sing something special for the midnight mass." Franz had blinked in disbelief at what he had just heard and was about to voice his protest when the priest shyly handed a piece of paper to Franz, saying, "I have written a few short verses. Perhaps you could put them to music, Herr Gruber, so the boys could sing them at the conclusion of the service this evening."

Franz thought, "Write it during the day, rehearse it once that evening, and sing it later that same night for mass? Father Mohr is an optimistic fellow. But he is asking for a miracle!" Franz had so many misgivings about the whole notion he really didn't know quite where to begin stating his objections. So he had said nothing, merely nodding his head in apparent agreement with the plan.

Now as Franz sat by the tiny fire in his chilly room, he thought, "How can he really expect me to write a tune in one day and teach it in one rehearsal to the boys?" He had not even glanced at the paper that Father Mohr had given to him, and more or less out of curiosity his hands began probing through his various pockets to see whether he could find the verses. "Oh yes, now I remember. I put the paper in my coat pocket." He arose and walked toward the door and rummaged the pockets in his greatcoat until his fingers closed over the little piece of paper he sought.

Wearily sitting down again in his chair before the fire, he unfolded the paper and began to read the words:

> *Silent night, holy night!*
> *All is calm, all is bright*
> *Round yon virgin mother and child.*
> *Holy Infant, so tender and mild,*
> *Sleep in heavenly peace.*

Compared to the majesty of the Palestrina mass, which had been so carefully rehearsed, surely this was the sound of a tinkling cymbal! Groping with futility and frustration, his mind turned back to the night when Christ was born. Surely it must have been a silent night in the stillness of that blessed stable. And of all of the nights that had ever been or were yet to come, it must indeed have been a holy night. Serenity and an inexplicable glow would have come from the babe so tender and mild, cradled in the manger, and Mary would have smiled knowingly at the tiny form who slept in such heavenly peace!

Franz warmed to a glow that did not come from the feeble fire in the grate, and his eyes turned eagerly to the second verse. He knew from memory the words of the Christmas story as told by Luke. What a thrilling, breath-taking sight it must have been to the shepherds who quaked at the sight of the glories streaming from heaven afar! Franz suddenly felt filled with wonder and could almost hear the heavenly hosts sing, "Alleluia! Christ the Savior is born!"

Melodies that he had never heard before raced through his mind as Franz turned quickly to the third verse of Father Mohr's poem. Yes, just as Father Mohr had told the boys in the choir, Christmas is truly a time when we celebrate a love come down from heaven, love's pure light. And the radiant beams from the face of the holy child were truly like the rays of the sun, dawning with redeeming grace for all of humankind. This *was* the message of the Lord at his birth!

As he stared at the small piece of paper, the words suddenly swam out of focus, blurred by a mistiness in his eyes. Franz felt his breath coming in short gasps for a few moments. Then a warmth, peace, and calm such as he had never known before descended on him. "Here is the entire meaning of Christmas wrapped up in a few simple lines!" Franz sat for a few moments, basking in

the flushed glow of discovery, when a feeling of utter dismay swept over him. "How can I ever find music to adequately portray the beauty of such a song as this? Such words demand the genius and the majesty of a Beethoven, not merely the efforts of a humble schoolmaster from a tiny village far up in the mountains of Austria!"

Torn by the conflict that raged within him, Franz reread the lines that Father Mohr had written, more slowly this time, digesting every nuance of the beautifully crafted phrases and marveling at its utter simplicity and truth. Then very suddenly he knew! "These lovely lines would be lost on a Beethoven, childish to a master like Palestrina! These simple expressions of the grandeur of God need melodies equally as simple and direct as the words themselves!" Almost fearing what his feelings were telling him to do, he slowly rose from his chair, walked over to the desk, and picked up the guitar that he used to accompany the singing of the students at school.

Lovingly, his fingers strummed the circle of three simple chords, and in a voice quite unlike his usual robust tone when leading the singing in the schoolroom, Franz gently began to articulate a melody to accompany the beautiful words of "Silent Night." As he sang Franz closed his eyes, for he no longer needed to read the words from the paper, and his left hand seemed to find the chords without any conscious direction. Before he actually knew what had happened, Franz had sung the entire first verse from beginning to end! The beauty of the words, the melody, and the soft, vibrant chords seemed to linger like the haze on the mountains at the beginning of a day in autumn, tarrying as if loathe to leave the memory.

Finally Franz opened his eyes and returned to the small, familiar world of Oberndorff. Slowly he rose from his chair and made his way back over to the desk. Gently he laid his guitar to one side and looked for a piece of paper and a quill. Ever the schoolmaster, he wanted to get the melody inscribed on paper, lest it be lost forever. With a steady hand he drew five lines for a staff, laid down his ruler, and returned to the lines to inscribe a treble clef at the beginning of the staff.

16

Although he felt a certain umbrage at being compelled to adhere to the mechanical demands of notation, he knew that he must put the song in a key that the boys could sing easily, particularly if they were obliged to learn it in one rehearsal and then to perform it for the mass. He thought back to his experience of a few moments before and then suddenly knew that the seemingly automatic movement of his fingers on the frets of the guitar had been correct in the first place. He had played it in the key of C major. This would present no problems for his boys in terms of additional sharps and flats to worry about. Then too, the song just happened to fall within the range of the best sounds that the boys sang. So, the key of C it would be! Almost effortlessly the notes flowed from the quill to the paper until the song was complete.

Franz mused, "Now what about the second verse and the third verse? Should they have individual melodies or should I use the same melody for all three of the verses?" Franz seemed to understand music a little better with a guitar in his hand, so he laid the quill pen back on the desk and gently picked up his guitar. He played the same simple chords and hummed the melody, almost like a lullaby that a mother would sing to her infant child.

As he hummed he could almost hear the boys singing the new carol of Christmas in their beautiful, clear tones. As he listened a new sound seemed to come forth; the whole song was in two-part harmony! Franz laid the guitar down carefully on the edge of the desk and peered at the notes he had written. "Why, yes. The contra altos could sing the same basic melody three notes lower than the sopranos and still not have a lot of difficult intervals to learn! He picked up his quill again and began to ink in the harmony, three notes below the melody line.

Franz suddenly felt filled with wonder and could almost hear the heavenly hosts sing, "Alleluia! Christ the Savior is born!"

His thoughts were interrupted by a soft knock at the door. Franz sighed at this earthly interruption to his divine communion, but made his way to the door. Upon opening it, he was greeted with a "Merry Christmas" from Otto Kleinkopft, who stood with a large plate of freshly baked treats in his hands. "Mama and Papa wanted me to bring these things over for your Christmas Eve dinner, Herr Gruber," he said and shyly extended the gift towards Franz. Herr Gruber was a little taken aback, but managed to mumble a word of thanks. Then Otto gravely inquired, "Are we still going to have choir rehearsal after dinner tonight, Herr Gruber?"

"There's no such thing as a secret in a small town," thought Franz. "Of course by now everyone in the village must know the organ doesn't work." But he turned to Otto and smiled, "Yes, indeed, Otto! I am sure all of the boys know we cannot use the organ tonight, but we shall have a wonderful Christmas in spite of it all!"

Otto looked puzzled, for he well knew Herr Gruber was a very thorough person who would not present anything in public unless it had been well rehearsed and polished to perfection. Otto persisted, "But Herr Gruber! In one rehearsal?"

Franz smiled again and said, "Just you and the rest of the boys be there at the church for choir rehearsal at the usual hour, and I'll have a surprise for all of you!" After Otto had gone, Franz was quite surprised when he looked out the window and discovered that the sun had fallen behind the peaks. Night would soon be upon them. It also came to his attention that he had not bothered to eat anything since breakfast and was very hungry. Franz thought, "How good it was of Herr Kleinkopft to have sent over the plate of sweetbreads." Franz greatly enjoyed his evening meal, augmented by the goodies from the bakery.

As he made his way down the stairs and through the village streets towards the church, he noticed the wind and snow had stopped. Instead of the cold, a beautiful warm glow permeated his whole being. His feet felt as light as his heart as he made his way through the deep snows of the Tyrolean winter night, and he quickly found himself at the church door. He placed his guitar on one of the choir pews, lit the candles in the sanctuary, and busied himself stoking the fire in the big stove at the rear of the church.

Just as he was finishing with the stove, the first of the boys arrived, excited as a young lad could be on Christmas Eve and bubbling over with news about the Christmas preparations at his home. This was multiplied many times over as each of the boys arrived, each with his own story to tell to the others. As soon as all of the boys were assembled, Herr Gruber took his place in front of the choir and gently tapped on the music rack to gain their attention. Despite the fact that Franz was their schoolmaster, as well as their choirmaster, it appeared that no one had heard the tapping, for the sounds of their boyish voices continued to fill the church with excited tones.

Franz tapped a little more sternly and little by little the conversations ceased as happy, excited eyes turned toward him. Franz began, "As all of you boys know, the mice have enjoyed their Christmas dinner a little early this year. They have eaten so many holes in the organ bellows that it will not work. So, unfortunately, all of the time and effort that we put into the Palestrina mass is for nothing!"

Franz paused a moment to let this thought sink in. As the faces of the boys began to grow a bit more somber, Franz smiled, much to the surprise of the boys. Franz waited a moment or two to let the air of expectancy grow. Then he said, "Father Mohr thinks we should prepare some special music for the mass tonight, in spite of the fact that the organ is out of order." He waited again, noting the puzzled looks on the faces of his young singers. "So, tonight, right at the conclusion of the mass, we shall sing a new carol, one that has never been heard before!"

The boys in the choir reacted just as Otto Kleinkopft had, with a look of apprehension, deepening when they recalled how Herr Gruber had drilled them over and over on the Palestrina mass. How could he ask them to rehearse something once and then to sing it during the service?

As if to answer the unspoken questions, Franz walked over to where he had laid his guitar and with absolutely no explanation strummed a few chords and began to sing the words that had so deeply moved him. As the last notes of the final verse faded away, a reverent hush (something not at all typical of the boys) filled the room. As Franz looked up from his guitar, he noted the vast silence together with tear-stained cheeks and trembling lips. Franz knew at once the boys loved the song as much as he did when it was first brought into being.

The remainder of the rehearsal was unlike any rehearsal Franz had ever directed. The boyish pranks, the talking, the inattention, the incessant giggling over anything or nothing were forgotten.

Later that evening, as the magic hour of midnight drew closer, the good folk of the village and the nearby farms began to make their way to the church. Looking out over the snowclad mountains of the Tyrol, Franz could see lanterns with their fresh candles bobbing like fireflies on a sea of white coming ever closer. The fire in the big stove at the rear of the church crackled audibly as the worshipers quickly came in and shut the door against the Alpine winter. They blew out their candle lanterns, set them to one side, and put their heavy wraps on the pegs at the back of the church.

Quietly, they made their way to their accustomed pews and knelt to pay their individual homage to the newborn King. Then Father Mohr began the mass and Franz thought even Palestrina could not have written anything more beautiful than the eternal words of the mass as spoken by that small congregation of country folk. Father Mohr had been quite correct about the carols. Franz had only to get his pitch from the pitchpipe and begin the carols that they all knew and loved for the little church to ring with the happy sound of voices celebrating the nativity. Franz heard very little of Father Mohr's sermon, however, for his thoughts strayed to the broken organ and to the wonder that had been born that day. In the warm, rosy light of the candelabra, Franz noted the glow of happiness that shone as brightly as the candles themselves as each of the parishioners filed to the altar to receive Christmas communion.

At last the time had come. As Father Mohr pronounced the anticipated "Missa est," Herr Gruber motioned for the boys of the choir to stand and reached for his guitar. Franz lovingly stroked the guitar, playing a few chords to set the key and the tempo of the long-awaited carol. Then the boys of the choir began to sing. In the warmth and radiance of the candlelight reflected in the simple decorations in the church, the song began as quietly as its name and swelled to a sound as majestic as that of the angelic hosts on the night when Christ was born. Simply and fervently the boys retold the beautiful story in the words crafted by Father Mohr.

As the last notes of "Silent Night" faded into the Austrian night, there was a hush as if the whole world had grown breathless with delight in the fact of the nativity. No one in the church stirred, fearful to break the magical spell that had been woven by the words and music. Men, strong from work in the fields, put their arms around their children in wordless thanksgiving. And all silently expressed their gratitude for the baby who had again entered their lives. Although Father Mohr was supposed to give the benediction, he sat quietly, not even aware he had any further obligations in the service.

There was a hush as if the whole world had grown breathless with delight.

Finally, the boys in the choir reverently began to file out of the choir stalls, each pausing long enough to smile at Franz as they passed. They joined the congregation, which quietly moved to gather their wraps, light the candles in their lanterns, and make their way to the door.

Quite suddenly, both Franz and Father Mohr realized they were alone. Together they moved to the open door of the church and watched the tiny candle lanterns bobbing up and down in the Christmas night, leading farther and farther into the darkness. Franz was almost startled by the voice of Father Mohr, a voice he scarcely recognized with its three short words: "Merry Christmas, Franz!" And to Franz Gruber, the quiet schoolmaster so far from home at Christmastime, it was, indeed, a very merry Christmas!

Shepherds' Song

WILLIAM R. MITCHELL

Dear little mother, we have come
    only to behold.
We will not touch his lovely face—
    our hands are rude and cold;
and we were only watching sheep
    huddled against the snow,
where David waited for the dawn
    ten thousand griefs ago;
and one was searching in the wilds
    a lamb that strayed apart,
stumbling through wearisome ravines
    anxious and sick of heart;
and one was making shelter
    for a labor-burdened ewe,
a warmth where she might lay her young
    (as all good shepherds do);
and I was listening to the flocks,
    like wildered children, plead
in almost human voices
    their almost human need;
and I was speaking comfort
    in the lonely, bitter night
(as shepherds must) when suddenly
    the skies were burst with light;
and the old, old hills of Judea
    and the cold of a thousand years
were laden with joy and singing
    and so we forgot our fears
and we kneeled down on the barren ground
    and shouted and laughed in our tears;
and so we have come to Bethlehem
    to wish our Savior well.
But why the cheeriest winter-song
    that ever men befell
should come to shepherds in the fields,
    Lady, we cannot tell.

Christmas Carol Greetings

BY RICHARD HILLERT

AMONG THE FASHIONS of Christmas that have acquired indisputable places in contemporary Christian custom are the sending of personal greetings and the singing of Christmas carols. The majority of people send professionally crafted Christmas cards. But the practice of sending personally designed Christmas letters is growing in many homes.

A special type of Christmas greeting has begun to appear with increasing frequency, combining something of the Christmas carol tradition with that of the homemade Christmas letter. Especially fortunate are those who have friends with the creativity to compose their yuletide greetings. The five carols that follow were written as Christmas greetings. They illustrate some of the variety and liveliness that naturally occur when expressing the sentiments of the season.

Few friends will claim the inspiration of the legendary German monk who had a vision of angels inviting him to dance and sing with them, and who upon awakening wrote down both the German and Latin words, as well as the tune, for *In dulci jubilo,* "Good Christian Friends, Rejoice." Rather, the qualification for writing a carol greeting would seem to be quite simple: the warm desire to express personal Christmas greetings to friends in a creative way. The circumstance of Martin Luther's writing and composing of "From Heaven Above" resembles that of a carol greeting. That hymn-carol was written for the children of his household as a 15-verse dialog between an angel and shepherds, retelling in song the first announcement of the birth of Christ.

The subject matter of the carol greeting can run the gamut of traditional carols: carols of Christmas night and stars, lullabies and cradle songs, songs of Christmas trees, of angels and shepherds, and wishes for peace on earth and happiness of the season. Someone inclined to write a carol text might start by writing new words to an already existing and well-known (or not so well-known) carol melody. Adding a new text to an old tune can make a legitimate, personalized greeting without confronting friends with something wholly strange and new.

Likewise, an equally creative greeting might be to write new music for an already existing text. Many of our well-known carol melodies were invented in that way. The words for "Hark! The Herald Angels Sing," for example, were written 100 years before the famous melody we know. The musical style employed in a new carol melody would, ideally, be primarily expressive of the words, whether lively or somber, mysterious or quietly lyrical. But again the emphasis in a personalized carol greeting is not on the musical artistry so much as on the warmth of friendship and the sheer urgency of personal expression conveyed through the words and music.

Collaboration between a poet and composer is always possible. But a new carol can be just as interesting and expressive when the author and composer are the same person, as can be seen in the selection of carol greetings that follow. It is by such creativity, whether done on commission from a great cathedral or for the simple purpose of wishing friends to have themselves "a merry little Christmas" with a few gentle reminders of the real meaning of this holy season, that the art of the carol and of the Christmas greeting is kept alive and lively.

Over the Plains of Bethlehem

Doris Grimstvedt Larsen   Doris Grimstvedt Larsen

1. O - ver the plains of Beth - le-hem, To his cra - dle
2. "Peace on earth, good will to men," Is the good news they're
3. En - ter our hearts, dear Lord, this night As we, our need con -

low ~ ly   Came the shep ~ herds from their fields,
bring ~ ing.   Sleep, my child, the Sav-ior is come,
fess ~ ing,   Know that with your Gift di - vine

Prais-ing his name most ho - ly. Wise men a - far were
Church bells the tid - ings are ring-ing. Wise men a - far were
We are all things pos - sess-ing. Wise men a - far were

led by the star To tell the won ~ drous sto - ry.
led by the star And tell hearts in joy are sing-ing.
led by the star That all may know his bless-ing.

Hush, My Babe

Elizabeth Isaak Paul

Elizabeth Isaak Paul

Hush, my babe, child of love. An-gels guide stars a-bove. Men shall seek thee

through the night,   led by hosts of heav'n-ly light. Wait, thou child, whose

light has come that all man-kind u-nite as one. White, red, and black,

yel-low, brown, all are chil-dren of thy crown. Sleep now, child, for

soon will come a world that can-not live as one. Give to them un-

shroud-ed sight of this peace-ful night.

23

Whisper, Hush!

Lois Rehder Holmes

Lois Rehder Holmes

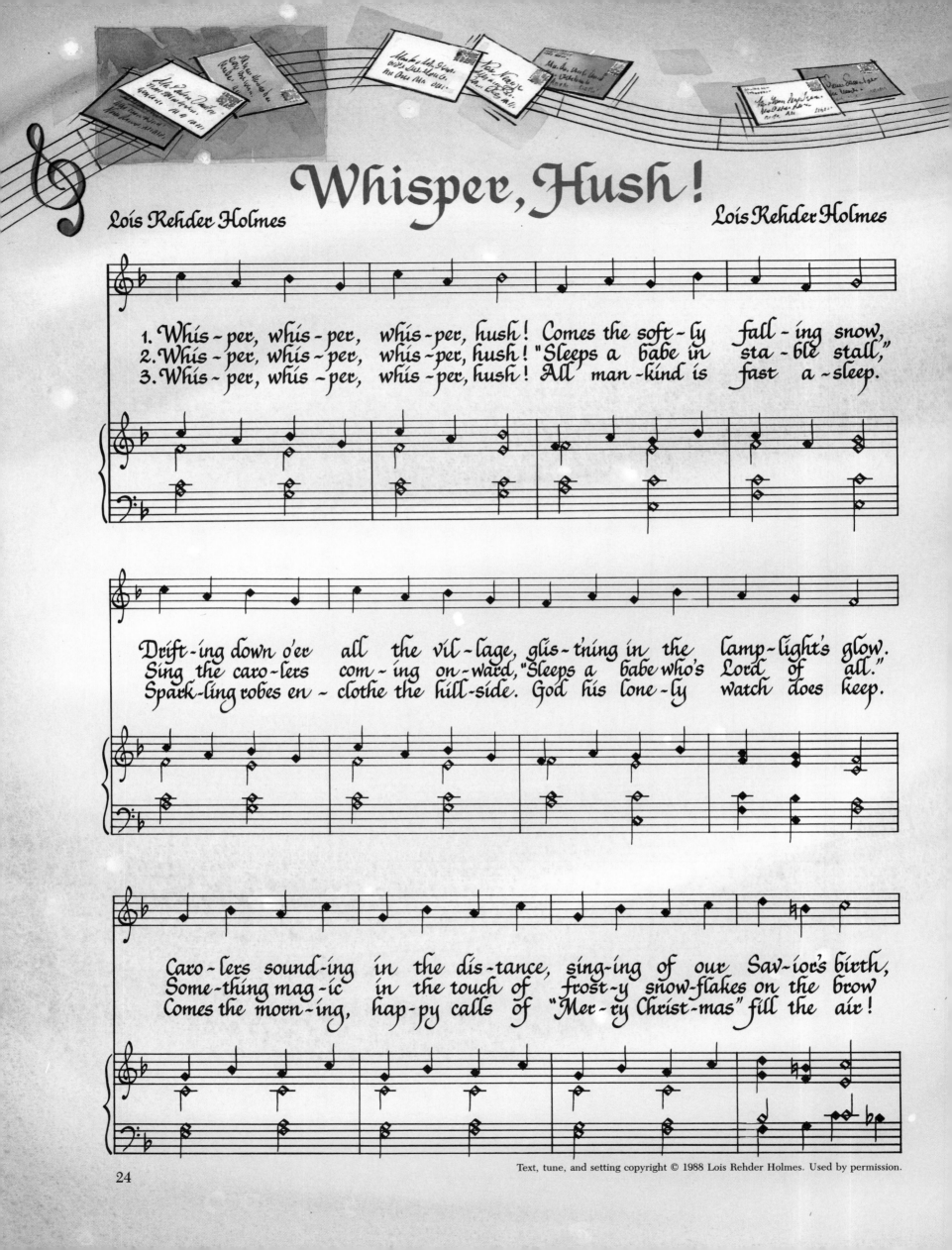

1. Whis-per, whis-per, whis-per, hush! Comes the soft-ly fall-ing snow,
2. Whis-per, whis-per, whis-per, hush! "Sleeps a babe in sta-ble stall,"
3. Whis-per, whis-per, whis-per, hush! All man-kind is fast a-sleep.

Drift-ing down o'er all the vil-lage, glis-'tning in the lamp-light's glow.
Sing the caro-lers com-ing on-ward, "Sleeps a babe who's Lord of all."
Spark-ling robes en-clothe the hill-side. God his lone-ly watch does keep.

Caro-lers sound-ing in the dis-tance, sing-ing of our Sav-ior's birth,
Some-thing mag-ic in the touch of frost-y snow-flakes on the brow
Comes the morn-ing, hap-py calls of "Mer-ry Christ-mas" fill the air!

Ech ~ o forth the song the an ~ gels first did sing to men on earth.
Makes hearts cheer ~ ful, spir ~ its warm, as man be ~ fore a child does bow.
Caro ~ lers come and swell the cho ~ rus, tell the good news ev ~ 'ry-where!

Unto Us a Child Is Born

Harry N. Huxhold

Paul Manz

Un-to us a child is born, Born of vir-gin ten-der, Born with-out a

roy-al crown, Laid with-in a man-ger. Glo-ry to the new-born child!

Winter Night Manger

Albert Rykken Johnson

Albert Rykken Johnson

1. In-fant lay on the hay in a sta-ble rude, Mo-ther there
2. Star at night by its light guides to paths all new; Hum-bly turn,

kneels in prayer, seek-ing ev-'ry good. Gift of love from a-bove
meek-ly learn what this child can do; Find this child deep in-side,

to man-kind be-low Who be-lieves and re-ceives finds the heart a-
hold him ev-er true; Let him grow, ev-er know

glow. Peace from God to you! Peace from God to you.

Not Just Another Day

JERRY MARTINO

I HAD JUST TURNED seven that spring in the late 1950s when John and Annie Burke moved into the house back of us. John was a retired railroader; a tall, spare old man who walked with a slight limp, the result of a fractured leg. Annie was a tall, stout woman with beautiful dark, wavy hair only slightly touched with gray, which she wore in a big coil on top of her head. Her most striking feature were her deep blue eyes, which contrasted with her milky skin.

I was a friendly child, so I decided to go over and get acquainted with our new neighbors. They saw a little tomboy, I think, for I always dressed in a T-shirt and jeans. My long hair I wore in two braids down my back. At first the Burkes were aloof and quiet. It never occurred to me that I might have been unwelcome. So I continued to visit, and gradually they warmed up. By summer, we three were chatting like old friends.

One hot day Annie and I were sitting in the swing on the front porch when I asked her if she had any children. It was a long while before she spoke. Then she said. "I had two children, but they both are dead. My little boy was named Francis, and he was so pretty and smart. He died when he was six, right before Christmas. He had diphtheria. My daughter was named Florene. She lived to grow up and get married, but then she got tuberculosis and died out at the sanitarium at Norton."

To my horror, Anne began to cry. I started to cry too. Putting my arms around her, I begged her not to cry. She dried her eyes on her apron and managed a smile.

"There, Jerry," she said, "I didn't mean to make you feel bad." She patted me on the shoulder and then straightened up and said, "Come with me. I'll show you some of their things."

Anne led me to the back bedroom, opened an old trunk, and lifted out a Celluloid box. It was ivory-colored with painted flowers on the top. She handed it to me, saying, "That was Florene's jewelry box." Then she lifted out a little iron bank in the shape of a steam locomotive and a small iron lantern like those railroaders carried. It

27

was full of miniature candies. "I got these for Francis' Christmas presents," she said. "But he died before I could give them to him. I've never opened the candy." I held each item a minute, then gave them back to her. She placed them in the trunk and closed the lid.

I often thought of Francis and Florene. But after school started, I didn't visit the Burkes as often. Then it seemed Christmas came with a rush! Stores in our village put up Christmas decorations, and the big star on top of the water tower was lit every evening. We got our Christmas things from their place on the top shelf of the clothes closet and set the nativity figurines on the bookcase.

I was still going over to see Annie and John after school when I could, and I noticed they had made no preparations for the holiday. I thought they might just be slow, for our family did not have a tree yet either. A few days before Christmas, however, we got our tree and trimmed it. Then we put lights in the window, and the whole house radiated the Christmas spirit. Still nothing was changed at the Burkes' house. Finally, on Christmas Eve, I could stand it no longer. I went over and asked Annie if she wasn't having a Christmas tree.

"No, honey," she said with a sigh. "We don't get much or give much at Christmas. For us, it's just another day."

Just another day! I hurried home and had a good cry. Mother comforted me. "Don't cry," she said. "You can do something to make the Burkes' Christmas happy. Take Annie that Santa you made at school and help her put it in the window. Then go up to Hazel Strode's Variety and get a little present for each of them. We have an assortment of Italian Christmas goodies ready, so I'll fix a plate of them for you to give."

I trotted over and took the Santa. "This is to go in your window," I said. "Here, I'll help you."

My next stop was the variety store where I bought a small bottle of shaving lotion for John and a bottle of perfume with a flashy bow on it for Annie. Taking my purchases home, I wrapped them with lots of tape and stickers. Then, gifts in hand, I marched over to Annie's and John's house. When I presented the things, my friends were stunned. "Why, Jerry, you didn't need to do this," they kept repeating. But I noticed how they smiled at each other.

Later that afternoon, I spotted John limping jauntily home with a little Christmas tree over his shoulder. I could hardly believe my eyes! What was happening? I found out a couple of hours later. I was playing in our backyard when Annie came to her kitchen door and called me to come over. She led me into the living room.

The little tree stood in the corner, trimmed with strings of popcorn and cranberries. Hanging on it were the two packages I had given them. On the table by the tree sat the plate of Christmas confections. In the window was the Santa I had made at school.

I clapped my hands and yelled, "You are ready for Christmas after all!" Annie and John smiled broadly.

"No, honey," she said with a sigh. "We don't get much or give much at Christmas. For us, it's just another day."

Then John said, "Look under the tree. There is something for you."

Looking under the tree, I found the jewelry box, the bank, and the lantern. "But those things belong to Francis and Florene," I protested.

Annie picked them up and placed them in my hands. "They're yours now, Jerry," she said. Then both of my friends hugged me close. "God bless you," Annie added. "You have given Christmas back to us."

That's the Christmas I'll never forget. Each year I live it all over again when I set up my Christmas tree. Underneath it I place the jewelry box, the bank, and the lantern still full of candy.

Traditions in Common

PATRICIA HADDOCK

There is a striking similarity in the kinds of Christmas traditions that have developed around the world. In almost every country where the birth of Christ is celebrated, certain customs have emerged: the baking of special holiday sweets, the singing of Christmas carols, the re-creation of the nativity scene, the use of candles, and the gathering of the family for a feast of holiday fare, to name a few. What makes the study of Christmas customs so intriguing are the delightful variations of these common traditions from one country to the next. Some of these variations are described in the pages that follow.

Cookies in Germany

Cookies and Christmas go together. While some German families buy their Christmas cookies ready-made, many bake their treats themselves, using recipes handed down through generations. The coffee table groans under the weight of cinnamon stars, hazelnut-almond-walnut biscuits, honey cakes, spice biscuits, macaroons, oatmeal biscuits, rum truffles, marzipan, and gingerbread.

Recipes and bakeware vary from region to region and even from town to town, leading to a remarkable variety of cookies and cakes throughout the country. Many of today's favorite cookies originated in the Middle Ages, when they were given as gifts.

Spekulatius and *Springerle*, while often machine-made today, originally were molded in traditional forms depicting elaborate scenes of St. Nicholas, animals, birds, guild workers, and country life. The biscuit molds were hollowed out from pear or cherry wood by woodcarvers, then the cookie dough was pressed into the hollows. Just carving the molds was a full-time occupation for an artisan; and carving the molds was recognized as an art form from the 13th century until the mid-1850s, when it died off.

Original molds are rare and valuable, often bequeathed as family heirlooms. But modern bakers who want to make these cookies can purchase metal molds in the traditional shapes.

Caroling in Puerto Rico

Navidades, the Christmas/Epiphany season in Puerto Rico, is marked by caroling of all kinds.

The Mass of the Carols, *Misas de Aguinaldo*, begins the festivities on December 16 at 5:30 A.M. Before dawn each day until Christmas, the devout attend church services. These services are marked by robust caroling. After mass, the celebrants carry the joy of the season with them by continuing to sing all the way to their homes and workplaces.

The music and carols don't stop with the Christmas Eve mass, called *Misa de Gallo*, but continue until January 6, the Epiphany. This is *the* big festival, and each town and village celebrates in its own traditional way. In Aguas Buenas, south of San Juan, celebrants gather before a painting of the Magi and sing carols. In San Juan, townspeople parade through the streets, which are gaily decorated with poinsettias and gold ribbons.

The highlight of the festivity is the *parrandas*. Neighbors go from house to house, playing guitars and serenading occupants. The hostess traditionally greets each visitor with a special song called a *copla*, which she improvises as each guest arrives. Visitors and householders end the visit with traditional carols and a toast for the season and friendship. The celebrants go off to the next house, where the singing, caroling, and toasting begin again. The *parrandas* continue until dawn, when the Christmas season comes to an end.

30

Family Feast in Denmark

Christmas in Denmark is marked by the most important family feast of the year on December 24. Even the family farm animals receive extra attention and food for the holiday, and wild birds feast on the bunches of grain left out for them.

Chiming bells summon everyone to church services on Christmas Eve afternoon. After services, the family returns home to begin the Christmas Eve feast.

The traditional entree is roast goose or duck stuffed with fruit and accompanied by sugar-browned potatoes, red cabbage, and berry jelly. A special treat, a rice porridge with whipped cream and chopped almonds, is made with one whole almond hidden inside. The person who finds the almond keeps it secret until all the healthful porridge is eaten. The winner then claims his or her prize for the almond—a piece of marzipan fruit.

After supper, each person goes to the head of the house and thanks him or her for the meal. Then the living room doors are opened to reveal the elaborately decorated Christmas tree surrounded by gifts. Everyone joins hands and dances around the tree, singing each person's favorite Christmas carol.

After the caroling, *Julemand*, a family member dressed as Santa, arrives and passes out the presents. The evening's festivities are capped with Danish Christmas cookies called *pebernødder* and *vejner.*

Creche in Italy

Italian Christmas celebrations start with a *novena*, nine days of prayers. On the first day of the *novena*, each family sets up a *praesepio* or manger scene in its home. Some *praesepios* are elaborately designed, with angels suspended overhead and an entire miniature village laid out surrounding the lowly inn. The tiny handcarved or cast nativity figures are often passed down through generations of family members.

The manger scene may also be set up on the bottom shelf of a pyramid-shaped display gaily decorated with pinecones, candles, and colorful paper. This is called a *ceppo* and may take the place of a Christmas tree. Every morning, the family begins the day by gathering around the manger scene for prayers.

Francis of Assisi created the first manger scene on a hillside outside of Greccio, Italy, in the thirteenth century. Francis wanted to bring alive the humility of Christ's birth for his ill-educated people. So he converted a cave on a hillside into a manger using a live ox and ass. Costumed villagers represented Mary and Joseph and the other members of the nativity story. This first manger scene so moved all who saw it that the custom rapidly spread and today the *praesepio* (or the *crèche*, as it is also commonly called) plays a major role in the Christmas celebrations of most Christian cultures. It is still the focal point of an Italian Christmas.

Candles in Sweden

December 13 marks the beginning of the Swedish Christmas season with the feast of Santa Lucia.

On the morning of December 13, one of the daughters in each family dresses as Santa Lucia in a white gown with a red sash. She wears a garland of green lingonberry leaves crowned with lighted candles. She sings the old Neapolitan hymn, *Santa Lucia,* and takes coffee and freshly baked saffron buns, called *Lusse Cats,* to her parents in their room. Any other girls in the family also dress in white and accompany Santa Lucia with lighted candles. Sons play a part in the family procession too, wearing tall, cone-shaped hats decorated with stars.

There are several legends about Lucia. According to one, she was a fourth-century Sicilian girl who was engaged to a pagan noble. She gave her dowry to the poor, and when her fiance accused her of being a Christian, she was sentenced to burn at the stake. But the flames did not harm her body and Lucia died only after being stabbed through with a sword. Another legend places Lucia in the Middle Ages where she brought food and hope to the starving people of Sweden. Regardless of which legend people believe, Santa Lucia is a symbol of hope and light.

The feast of Santa Lucia marks the day when all the planning for Christmas must be completed. Candles and household decorations are ready and the baking is finished in anticipation of Christmas Day.

A Different Kind of Christmas

KATHLEEN R. RUCKMAN

THE TINY VILLAGE of Velky' Slavkov lay nestled in the foothills of the High Tatra Mountains in eastern Czechoslovakia. The Danube River rippled smoothly nearby and the sky shone a brilliant blue against the massive, snow-capped mountains. Above the village row upon row of tall, dense pine trees were blanketed in the sheer silk of a morning vapor. And behind the trees rose rugged mountain peaks crowned in dazzling white.

The year was 1910. A plague overshadowed the village. How could such a lovely place harbor an epidemic that threatened the very lives of its people? "Don't go near *that* house!" children would squeal as they walked to the old village school just two days before Christmas. A black "X" on the wooden doorposts marked the many quarantined homes, their shades solemnly pulled and shutters tightly closed.

Once rosy-cheeked and robust in their peasant skirts and bonnets, many women lay sick and helpless. Men, once hardy workers in the fields, lay dying in a feverish state, gasping for that clean mountain air no longer theirs. Children too were innocent victims of a monster that would soon swallow them up. Diphtheria had descended on Velky' Slavkov.

Susan, the only healthy one in the Boratkova household, kneeled at her doorpost weeping and praying in Slovak. Her husband, John, could be heard from the woodshed where he was pounding the last nail into the coffin he had built for their two little sons. John was not only weeping but was also wheezing, for he too had diphtheria. First their daughter, Mary, had died one week before Christmas. Then, just two days before the blessed holiday, their sons, John and Paul, had died within 24 hours of each other. Susan and John were childless.

Situated in east central Europe, Czechoslovakia has known a succession of governments. The three regions of Czechoslovakia—Bohemia, Moravia, and Slovakia— were all part of the ninth century Moravian Empire.

Then in 1918, under the direction of both Czech and Slovak leaders, the Republic of Czechoslovakia was formed. But 20 years later Hitler's troops occupied the land, and the government was dissolved. Bohemia and Moravia were made protectorates of Germany; while Slovakia was declared independent in 1939. Soviet troops entered Czechoslovakia five years later and seized power in 1948. An attempt at liberalization was made in 1968, but this was quickly squelched by an invasion of Russian, Polish, East German, Hungarian, and Bulgarian armies. Now, as part of the Communist bloc, Czechoslovakia leads the eastern Europe countries in industry and technology.

Susan, sobbing in agony, cleaned and wrapped her baby sons and carefully laid them in the simple pine box. She and John then lifted it onto the wagon, where the old workhorse stood ready to pull two more victims of the terrible calamity. Driving the wagon through knee-high snow, John and Susan braced themselves against the chilling wind that stung both body and soul.

"Another trip to the graveyard is more than I can bear!" cried Susan as they passed house after house marred by the black death mark. Susan and John knew the agony and empathized with those families, but they didn't have the strength to offer sympathy or encouragement. It took all of their energy just to bury their own children and somehow see John through his illness.

All three of their children now slept under a blanket of earth and snow. Susan, struggling through the Lord's Prayer, hugged the cold ground and wouldn't let go. John finally pulled her away with what little strength he had and led her back to the wagon. She clutched her empty arms and crossed them over her broken heart, never to hold her babies again.

It was dusk and tomorrow would be Christmas Eve. As John and Susan entered their barren and branded house, they needed comfort. They needed village friends and church folk. But no one dared come near. There were no Christmas greetings, no sympathies extended.

Nearly wiped out in 1910 by an epidemic of diphtheria, the Boratkova family was saved by a mysterious gypsy woman. This visa photo of Susan and her children was taken shortly before they left Czechoslovakia to join John in America. Their ship reached Ellis Island on February 22, 1926.

Left to right: Julia (a twin) holding John (a triplet); Susan (mother) holding Robert (a twin); Samuel and Paul in the center (two of the triplets); Ann (a singleton) holding Bartholomew (twin to Robert); and Andrew (twin to Julia). Another little girl, Helen (not shown), was born in America.

The black "X" spelled DEATH and DO NOT ENTER. Their house was like a frightful, forbidden tomb.

Little high-laced leather shoes stood lined up against the woodstove, just as they usually did after the children were tenderly tucked into bed. But now, the fluffy feather bed was empty. Never had the old house felt so cold.

"I won't see another Christmas," John whispered weakly. "I don't think I'll see this new year either."

He pushed away the soup and bread he could not swallow. It was as though the enemy diphtheria had tied a noose around John's throat, allowing neither food nor sufficient air to sustain him.

Susan gathered kindling and made a fire for the night, then sat down to await her husband's death. Morning came and it was Christmas Eve. Snowflakes fell from a swollen gray sky and the wind blew a white mist over the already frosted windowpanes. Susan, tired from a night without sleep, dipped her cloth again in cold water to help cool John's burning fever. Then rubbing the icy glaze off her lattice window, she fixed her eyes on the Tatra Mountains and quoted the psalm, "I will look to the hills from whence cometh my help."

Suddenly, her gaze was interrupted by the sight of a gypsy woman trudging through the snow. The red and purple plaid woolen shawl draped over the gypsy's stout shoulders hardly seemed warm enough as its crocheted lace trim dangled loosely. Her babushka, or kerchief, hugged a red face raw from the wind. Her full peasant skirt was a display of cotton and linen patchwork in all colors of the rainbow. Woolen leggings and high-buttoned boots allowed her to plod through the snow and over the frozen earth. Susan stood half-stunned and motionless as the old woman shuffled up the forbidden walkway, holding in her uncovered hands a jar of clear liquid.

The knocker on the weather-beaten door struck twice before Susan opened it to a most unusual face. This face, wrinkled from many summers in the searing sun and an equal number of severe winters, expressed the serenity of a calm in the storm. Her eyes were as blue as the Danube River when reflecting the sky on a clear day and shone with a depth that reached to the gypsy's soul.

"We have the plague in our home, and my husband is in a fever right now," Susan warned her.

Taking the liberty to step inside the door out of the icy wind, the gypsy held out her little jar to Susan. "Take a clean white linen and wrap it around your finger," she instructed. "Dip your finger into this pure kerosene oil and swab out your husband's throat. Then have him swallow a tablespoon of the oil. This should cause him to vomit the deadly mucous membranes. Otherwise he will surely suffocate. I will pray for you and your family."

With that the gypsy turned and stepped outside, shielding herself against the whistling wind as she took a moment to squeeze Susan's hand. From her countenance flowed a mixture of love and sincerity. Never before had Susan's heart been so touched by another human being and by such love that took all risks and disregarded all rules to show that someone cared. Here was love offering itself to the outcast.

Susan stood speechless for a moment, watching the gypsy walk toward a village where there would be no Christmas singing. But a song arose in Susan's heart and she called out to the gypsy, "I'll try it! God bless you!"

By Christmas morning, John had retched up the deadly mucous membranes and his fever had broken. Susan wept and praised God in her Slovak tongue as a flicker of hope lightened her heart; surely God would bless her and John with more children someday.

It was a different kind of Christmas. There were no gifts under a trimmed and tinseled tree. But the gift of a small glass jar glimmering on the window sill reminded Susan of a gift offered long ago, a gift in an alabaster box that was spilled out and lavished on One who was despised and rejected. The gift of life in that jar lived on, not only in Susan and John but in generations to come.

Footnote: Susan and John lived for many more years. During those years, two sets of twins, a set of triplets, and two other children were born to them. Two of the triplet boys were named John and Paul, after the two who died from diphtheria. The other triplet was named Samuel and is the father of the author of this story.

36

The Birth of Our Savior

Nathaniel Currier (1813-1888)

PHILLIP GUGEL

THE BIRTH OF OUR SAVIOR is one of almost 400 lithographs of religious subjects known published by the New York firm of Currier and Ives between 1834-1907. Unlike a Rembrandt portrayal of the nativity done for a discerning patron appreciative of his artistic excellence, this Currier and Ives print was a popular art form sold to a largely unsophisticated, though admiring American public.

During the nineteenth century the development of lithography, a printmaking process based on the chemical principle that oil and water are mutually repellent, made such affordable pictures readily available. Producing them involved a team of artists, letterers, lithographers, and colorists.

After drawing a preliminary picture, an artist copied it on a printing stone, a thin, flat rectangle of smoothly polished limestone. The copying was done with a greasy liquid and had to be perfect, since it was difficult to make corrections. The stone was then moistened with water, treated with an acid solution, and rolled with an oily ink that adhered only to the drawing. One writer dubbed the ink Currier and Ives made a "witches brew" because of its odd concoction of beef suet, castile soap, gas black, goose grease, gum mastic, shellac, and white wax. Next, the inked stone was pressed against a sheet of paper, yielding a reverse image of that drawn on the stone. Lithography's advantages for printmaking included its easier and quicker process for preparing the printing stone and the large number of impressions that could be made at low cost.

With some exceptions, these lithographs were printed in black and white and then hand-tinted by young women who were "trained colorists." With a color model of the print as a guide, each woman applied one color to her copy and then passed it on to the next colorer. The colorers earned a penny for each print painted. Though a supervisor made a final check of each completed color copy and finished any difficult details, errors sometimes occurred, as in this copy of *The Birth of Our Savior*. Colors run over the babe's left arm and over the picture's margins in several places. Portions of the staffs held by Joseph and one of the shepherds are painted blue like their cloaks. Areas of the tree are unpainted.

Since we now take color pictures of any sort for granted, it may be difficult for us to understand the impression these lithographs made on the general public. Until late in the nineteenth century, the average American home had little color in its decor and furnishings. No magazines or newspapers with color pictures were in circulation. So the color imagery of these Currier and Ives prints became a key factor in their appeal to and purchase by people who wanted to enliven their walls with colorful pictures of popular interest.

The anonymous artist of *The Birth of Our Savior* took a somewhat different approach than that found in many renditions of the nativity in placing the holy family and shepherds away from the stable. Except for the animals, we see little of the traditional imagery found in scenes of the shepherds' visit. The scene focuses on the essentials and takes into account that its audience would not have understood much hidden symbolism. The bound lamb recalls certain biblical references to Jesus as the Lamb of God; while the form of the manger, which resembles an altar of sacrifice, alludes to the sacrificial nature to his life.

Some peculiarities are evident in the artist's rendition of certain figural features: the men's hands are too wide, their fingers become extremely tapered, and the young shepherd on the left kneels in an ambiguous position while having the appearance of a miniature adult. Artistic excellence was not the reason why this and other Currier and Ives prints sold well; their appeal came from their color and the subjects they illustrated.

Though it lacks the bold colors and subtle highlighting seen in many of the large-size Currier and Ives lithographs of life in the United States, the subdued colors and some skillful shading in *The Birth of Our Savior* have a pleasing effect. Probably printed between 1834 and 1856, it comes from the years when Nathaniel Currier was the firm's sole owner.

> Artistic excellence was not the reason why this and other Currier and Ives prints sold well.

In 1857 Currier made his brother-in-law, James Ives (1824-1895), who had worked with him since 1852, a partner. Drawing upon their printing and marketing talents, Currier and Ives soon became the best known and most successful nineteenth century lithographers. They published between seven to eight thousand known prints, which appealed to the broadest range of interests. Especially popular were their scenes of American life. And their methods of production and market distribution were decades ahead of their time. The lithographs were distributed through shops and street peddlers in the United States and also shipped to Europe through London. The small ones, such as *The Birth of Our Savior*, sold for 15 to 25 cents, while the large ones sold for $1.50 to $3.00.

As an expression of popular American religious art from the nineteenth century, *The Birth of Our Savior* offers a somewhat sentimental view of Jesus' birth. But its message to come and draw near the manger still stirs us as it did people then.

Pella Preserves Dutch Christmas

CAROL VAN KLOMPENBURG

Each December 5 the patron saint of Amsterdam, Sinterklaas, arrives by boat at the harbor, then rides through the streets of the Netherlands capital city astride a white horse. Dressed in a red velvet cape and bishop's miter, Sinterklaas occupies a dignified place in Dutch folk tradition. He is accompanied by black-faced Zwarte Piet (Black Peter) attendants and bears simple gifts—cookies and chocolate alphabet letters—which he distributes to children who have been good during the preceding year.

Sinterklaas has played a part in Dutch Christmas tradition for centuries. Each December 5 children throughout the Netherlands countryside perform a yearly bedtime ritual. On the table they set out a snack for Sinterklaas; near the fireplace they set their wooden shoes containing a bit of hay for his white horse. In the morning they find that Sinterklaas has eaten the snack and replaced the hay with a gift or two. Usually they find a Sinterklaas cookie, a piece of fruit, and perhaps a simple toy. When older children check their shoes, however, they find a piece of coal instead of a gift. This is the saint's way of telling them they are too old for a Sinterklaas gift. These children understand his message and never put out their shoes for Sinterklaas again.

An ocean away from Amsterdam, a United States Sinterklaas rides into the Iowa town of Pella each December, also dressed in a red velvet cape and astride a white horse. Three Zwarte Piet helpers walk alongside him carrying willow switches and rags, the switches to punish children who have misbehaved the previous year and the rags

to wipe away their tears. They distribute candies—anise, peppermints, and chocolates—to the mittened, hooded crowd. The children briefly bare their fingers to the cold to unwrap the candies, then sheath their hands again in fuzzy warmth.

The majestic figure of Sinterklaas, dressed in a rich red velvet cape and mitre trimmed with gold, can be seen riding through Pella, Iowa, on a white horse each December in keeping with the town's Dutch heritage.

Preserving Dutch traditions is important to Pella, a small community of 8000 in central Iowa. Founded in 1847 by a band of Dutch settlers who emigrated from the Netherlands to escape religious persecution, the town has retained its Dutch flavor in its 140-year existence. Windmills,

brick streets, tiled roofs, blue Delft, and Hindeloopen painting visible along the parade route testify to its heritage.

A small band playing Christmas carols and a bellringing town crier in a velvet jacket and britches precede Sinterklaas. The crier proclaims the arrival of the saint much as town criers did in early Dutch towns, walking through the cobblestone streets announcing community births, deaths, and meetings. Small children costumed as presents and a Christmas tree complete the parade.

The watching crowd is encouraged to welcome their visitor with a traditional song:

Sinterklaas kapoentje,
Gooi wat in mijn schoentje,
Gooi wat in mijn laarsje,
Dank U, Sinterklaasje.

Which translated means:

Sinterklaas, dear old man,
Put something into my shoe,
Put something into my boot,
Thank you, Sinterklaas.

The parade halts at the town square, Sinterklaas dismounts, and he and his company climb the steps of the Tulpen Toren (Tulip Tower), an outdoor stage beneath twin 70-foot pylons. The towers are linked at the top by a 13-ton casting of the Dutch House of Orange crest, painted in the royal colors of the Netherlands—red, blue, and gold. Beneath the crest is emblazoned the motto of William of Orange, *"Je Maintiendrai"* (I shall endure). The town regards this monument as a tribute both to its Dutch heritage and to the determination and fortitude of the pioneer spirit.

From the Tulip Tower stage Pella's mayor welcomes Sinterklaas, and the saint responds. The town crier

(**left**) *A crowd gathers to welcome St. Nicholas or Sinterklaas, as he is called, to their town. In Dutch tradition, St. Nicholas remains a bishop who comes bearing simple gifts every December 5 and 6. Showing a special interest in children, Sinterklaas awards each one a piece of candy, that is, if they've been good.*

(**right**) *A parade is held in honor of Sinterklaas' arrival. He rides through town on a white horse led by one of his helpers known as Zwarte Piet or Black Peter. Three Zwarte Piets accompany Sinterklaas through Pella. They carry switches and rags—the switches to punish those who have misbehaved the previous year and the rags to wipe away their tears.*

unrolls a yellowed scroll and reads Pella's official proclamation of Sinterklaas Day:

> Whereas Pella is proud of her heritage,
> and
> Whereas Dutch customs and traditions are meaningful to many of us,
> and
> Whereas Sinterklaas comes to visit Dutch boys and girls with treats and gifts each year in December,
> and
> Whereas we want the children of Pella to experience the fun and songs of Sinterklaas,
> I hereby proclaim today as Sinterklaas Day in Pella.

The crowd cheers and Sinterklaas again steps forward. He honors the children costumed as Christmas tree and gifts, awarding each a candy. He then surveys the crowd. Are there any children who have been naughty this year? He spots a few. The Zwarte Piets capture the erring children and imprison each in a large sack. Sinterklaas approaches the sacks.

"Do you promise to be good?" he questions sternly.

"Yes, yes, we will be good," the children promise, and they are set free from the sacks.

A children's choir performs a few Dutch songs and folk dances, and the *Burgemeester* (Honorary Mayor) relates a brief history of the Sinterklaas tradition.

Nicholas, who was later to become known as Sinterklaas, was born in the third century to a wealthy family in what is now Turkey. When his parents died in an epidemic, he gave his wealth to the poor and entered the priesthood. Early records show that as Archbishop at Myra he fought fearlessly for his beliefs, supervising the destruction of a pagan temple. He also stopped the execution of three innocent men, convincing the governor to set them free.

For several centuries Nicholas was not widely known. Then 500 years after Nicholas' death, St. Methodius, patriarch bishop of Constantinople, wrote a colorful and detailed account of Nicholas' life. That was the start of the legendary St. Nicholas.

His salvation of the three condemned men formed the pattern for many legendary rescued trios. In one story he saved three storm-tossed fishermen; in another he brought three murdered children

back to life. Yet another legend tells of a poor nobleman living near St. Nicholas whose three daughters were unable to marry because he could not give them a dowry. St. Nicholas, hearing of their plight, rode by and threw bags of money through an open window into their home. One bag landed in a stocking that was drying at the fireplace, and with that the Christmas stocking tradition had begun.

Within a century after St. Methodius' writing, St. Nicholas came to be revered in both Eastern and Western Europe. In the East he was considered the patron saint of sailors; in the West he was thought of as the children's saint. Greece and Russia adopted Nicholas as their patron saint, as did the Dutch seaport capital Amsterdam. In the twelfth and thirteenth centuries many churches were constructed in his honor.

On his feast day, December 6, Dutch children attending the St. Nicholas church schools held gift-giving parties in his honor. When talking about the saint, the children misspoke his name, and he became known as Sinterklaas. Parades, programs, and gift-giving parties gradually became part of the tradition.

When the Dutch first immigrated to the United States, they brought Sinterklaas with them. In the American tradition he underwent a metamorphosis, became Santa Claus and brought gifts on Christmas Eve. But in the Dutch tradition he remained a bishop who came bearing simple gifts on December 5 and 6. Dutch gift-giving occurs at this time, and Christmas Day is celebrated as a religious holiday only.

When the Pella *Burgemeester* finishes his brief history, the brass band plays a finale and the crowd disperses. Sinterklaas and his retinue retrace the parade route back to the Scholte Church for a party for members of the Pella Historical Society, which sponsors the parade.

The Scholte Church is a white frame building, a replica of the church built in 1855 by Hendrick Pieter Scholte. Scholte, the founder of Pella, was always known to his parishioners as "the Dominie." Entering the church, society members pass beneath a sign bearing Scholte's Latin motto, *In Deo Spes Nostra et Refugium* (In God is our strength and refuge). Accompanied by an old organ, they sing Dutch songs. Some who know the Dutch language sing full voice; others stumble laughingly along, mispronouncing the strange letter combinations. Although the songleader reads the stanzas aloud

before they are sung, it is easy to forget, for example, that *zijn*, pronounced correctly, rhymes with *rain*.

After the songs, Sinterklaas reads a Christmas folktale to the children seated around him on the floor of the nave. Then, peering at his huge, red book, he reads the name of each child present and one of the child's good deeds (secretly supplied earlier in the week by the child's parents). "Jonathan Vander Ploeg is a good cub scout," he reads. "Sylvia De Jong keeps her room neat. John Kuyper tells good jokes." He pauses after each name and his Zwarte Piet helpers award a gift-wrapped chocolate letter to each deserving child.

Until recently nearly all of Pella's residents were of Dutch descent. But now the Jaarsma, Vermeer, and Vander Leest names on the roster of Sinterklaas participants are joined by names like Shearer, Caldwell, and Birdsall. Some of the newcomers eventually come to regard themselves as "adopted Dutchmen."

The awards finished, the children troop downstairs for a party and puppet show, while the adults remain upstairs for more singing followed by traditional Dutch pastries—Sinterklaas cookies, *kletskoppen* (lace cookies), and *olie bollen* (doughnuts).

Dominie Scholte's ornate and dignified pulpit looms above all else.

(above) The Tulpen Toren or Tulip Tower is linked at the top by a 13-ton crest of the Dutch House of Orange, painted in red, blue, and gold—the royal colors of the Netherlands. The parade halts here and Sinterklaas dismounts and climbs the steps to the tower. There the mayor of Pella greets the saint, and Sinterklaas Day is officially proclaimed.

(right) Asking if any children have been naughty this year, Sinterklaas spots a few, whom the Zwarte Piets capture and imprison in large sacks. The children are released only after they promise to be good.

(opposite page) At Scholte Church, members of the Pella Historical Society gather for a party. They sing Dutch songs and listen as Sinterklaas, surrounded by children, reads a Christmas folktale. More gifts and refreshments of traditional Dutch pastries follow.

From this pulpit the Dominie would peer over his rimless spectacles at the Dutch pioneers and preach impassioned sermons, sometimes lasting several hours. The men of the congregation had the option of standing and stretching during the lengthy services. But the ladies, who were expected to remain seated, refreshed themselves by sniffing cologne.

In the 1830s and 1840s Dominie Scholte and other dissenters had separated from the Dutch state church and were forbidden to hold worship services. Because their continued meeting for worship resulted in imprisonment and economic hardship for them, they decided to emigrate, eventually choosing Iowa.

When Scholte and his 800 followers arrived on the Iowa prairie, by wagon or on foot, only a single log cabin greeted them. They named

their settlement Pella, recalling the city by that name in Asia Minor in which early Christians had found refuge from Roman persecution. When they platted the town they named the streets after steps in the Christian life: Entrance, Inquiry, Perseverance, Reformation, Gratitude, Experience, Patience, Confidence, Expectation, and Accomplishment.

Scholte's religious influence is still felt in Pella, and residents take their religious life seriously. On Sunday downtown Pella is quiet, as worshipers attend church, many attending both a morning and an evening service. Only a scattered gas station and restaurant are open for business. Pella newcomers, not accustomed to the stern Dutch sabbath, are taken aback when neighbors chide them for washing their cars or mowing their lawns on Sunday.

After arriving on the Iowa prairie

that August in 1847, the pioneers hurried to build themselves shelters before winter. Lumber was scarce, and some created dugouts in the prairie sod, weaving its long grasses into roofing for their crude shelters. Pella soon earned the laughingly applied nickname "Strawtown," a name still preserved in one of the town's restaurants, Strawtown Inn. Located in a restored, century-old brick building, the restaurant features Dutch cuisine in an old European atmosphere.

Many of the town's old homes have been preserved and restored. The most imposing of these is the 23-room Scholte mansion, built by the wealthy Dominie for his elegant bride Mareah the year after their arrival. Leonora Hettinga, a great-granddaughter of Pella's founder, occupies one wing of the home. The remainder is preserved as a museum, housing Scholte's library, Mareah's square piano, and all the family memorabilia.

Respect for the town's pioneer past and its Dutch heritage is part of Pella's life in the twentieth century. Each May, citizens celebrate a Tulip Festival, scrubbing streets in wooden shoes, lace hats, and long, aproned dresses. Thousands of visitors flock to the town to view the tulip beds that line the streets in a profusion of color. Visitors are also treated to a Volks Parade (People's Parade), and a chance to visit the Scholte home and to tour Pella's Historical Village.

The Historical Village, a complex of 17 buildings, features pioneer items such as a water-powered grist mill and a log cabin. It also houses Dutch memorabilia: an antique Delft collection, a Dutch costume display, and a bakkerij (bakery). During the Tulip Festival, the village is alive with crafts: Sinterklaas cookie baking, wooden shoe making, weaving, and candlemaking.

Pella's Tulip Festival Queen and Princesses also make their appearance at the December Sinterklaas celebration, circulating through the crowd and distributing candies. Both traditions show the town's respect for its heritage. Celebrating the arrival of Sinterklaas preserves a Dutch Christmas for Pella residents. In a wonderful way their colorful heritage becomes a part of their contemporary lives each December.

41

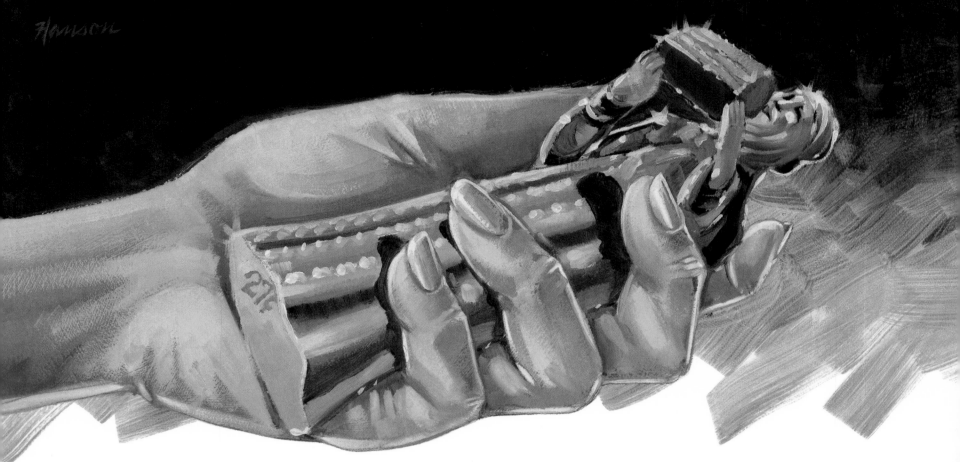

My 27-Cent Wise Man

LOUISE B. WYLY

WHAT TRADITIONS will you leave behind for your family? Do you have practices or beliefs that your children will cherish when they remember Christmas in your home? Will your grandchildren inherit these traditions?

As a seven-year-old, I had no intention of starting a tradition when I purchased a manger set at our local dime store. But I remember how very special it was to save up my nickels and dimes to buy that manger set. The entire set cost about three dollars, not much money by today's standards. But in 1939, three dollars seemed like a fortune to a seven-year-old.

This manger set consists of nine figures, all made of plaster and painted. My favorite piece to the set is one Wise Man. I call him my 27-cent Wise Man because he still has the original price, 27 cents, stamped clearly on the bottom.

Even after all these years, I'm still captivated by the story of the Wise Men, who knew enough to leave everything and follow the star until they found the newborn King. Maybe that's why they are called *wise* men!

Through the years, I've come to value this manger set purchased in a small town some thousand miles from the big city where I now live. My parents are gone and I seldom get back to my hometown in Pennsylvania. But my 27-cent Wise Man serves as a link from the past and a guide to the future. That small figure will serve as a witness to our family's trust in Christ from generation to generation, for it has become a tradition in our family.

In some families, traditions are carefully planned and established, then passed on to the next generation. In other families, traditions unexpectedly arise out of some special interest or event. Just so, no real planning went into establishing the Wise Man as a family tradition.

Each year, my husband and I would place the humble nativity set on a table in our living room. There it testified to all who entered of the real meaning of Christmas. It was given a central place in our home, reflecting the central place Christ held in our heart. Our children too learned to enjoy and respect the manger set as a special part of our family's celebration of Christmas. As they were growing up, our four children would beg over and over again to hear the story of how God sent his Son, Jesus, to earth to be our Savior. The children never tired of hearing it repeated.

Then we would all sing the carols that went with the Christmas story. When the angel spoke to the shepherds: "Behold, I bring you good tidings of great joy, which shall be to all people" (Luke 2:10), we would sing:

Silent night, holy night!
All is calm, all is bright
Round yon virgin mother and child.
Holy Infant, so tender and mild,
Sleep in heavenly peace,
Sleep in heavenly peace.

When we talked about how the shepherds came to Bethlehem to find the baby Jesus, we would sing:

Joy to the world, the Lord is come!
Let earth receive its King;
Let ev'ry heart prepare him room
And heav'n and nature sing,
And heav'n and nature sing,
And heav'n, and heav'n and nature sing.

It was our special privilege to teach our children about the joy that came to the world that night, that "silent night" when the shepherds were told about the Savior's birth.

Our children liked to move the figures around, yet they never broke a figure. Sometimes they would place the animals outside the stable; sometimes they would put them inside with the baby. Once they even left the baby outside, but not for long! Then our children would play school. Our oldest girl would ask the younger ones questions about Jesus' birth. They would pretend to be the cow or the sheep and answer her. Thus, the manger scene became a center for family learning.

I think the favorite part of the story to all the children was hearing that Jesus had no crib. One year we got some real hay and spread it out for the animals. This smelled sweet and reminded us of the hay on which Mary had laid her baby. The children could identify with this, for each one had a soft bed in which to sleep and could still remember when our youngest had slept in a crib.

Somehow my love for the Wise Men transferred to our children as well. They all loved to picture the Wise Men guided by God with one lone star all the way to Bethlehem. Together we would wonder how long it had taken them to travel so far on camels and imagine how hot the journey must have been. By the time the Wise Men reached Bethlehem, Jesus had grown to be a young child. He was no longer a tiny baby in Mary's arms; by then he could sit on Mary's lap.

Now each year at Christmastime we remember the Wise Men who brought gifts to Jesus. And as we open our gifts to one another, we remember the One who gave the supreme Gift of Jesus Christ: "For God so loved the world that he gave his only begotten Son, that whoever believes in him should not perish but have everlasting life" (John 3:16).

Just as the Wise Men, when they had presented their gifts, fell down and worshiped the Lord Jesus, so we desire to worship Jesus as our Lord and our God.

Recently, our oldest daughter asked us, "Could I have the manger set so I can carry on the tradition with my three children?" Her request brought joy to our hearts, knowing that our tradition would be passed on to another generation, to our grandchildren.

Giving the old set to our daughter didn't end the tradition in our home, however, for we replaced it with a new one. The new set didn't cost three dollars and it doesn't have a 27-cent Wise Man. But its message remains the same: "Joy to the world, the Lord is come!"

What a delight it is to see our grandchildren enjoy the same story as they ask us: "Grandma, tell us the story of your 27-cent Wise Man again" or "Grandpa, why didn't

As a seven-year-old, I had no intention of starting a tradition when I purchased a manger set at our local dime store. The entire set cost about three dollars.

the little Lord Jesus have a crib to sleep in?" And so with joy we pass on the special message: To you is born a Savior.

Then we sing with our children and grandchildren that treasured lullaby:

> *Away in a manger, no crib for his bed,*
> *The little Lord Jesus laid down his sweet head;*
> *The stars in the sky looked down where he lay,*
> *The little Lord Jesus asleep on the hay.*

We enjoy our grandchildren's questions as we remember how much this tradition has meant in our own family. We see what values this tradition has carried all these years and what it will teach to future generations. My 27-cent Wise Man emphasizes the true meaning of Christmas, which has been celebrated in our family for the past 30 years. Best of all, that little figure brings with him a part of the past from afar. He is a tradition in our family that has grown out of our shared love for the Savior he once journeyed to find.

NICHOLAS: From Saint to Santa Claus

CAROL L. MASTERS

LONG AGO IN PATARA, a village located in the country we now call Turkey, lived a couple named Epiphanes and Johane. They were members of the early Christian community. Barely 200 years earlier, their ancestors had been converted by the apostle Paul as he traveled and preached about Jesus in their country of Lycia.

Married for many years, Epiphanes and Johane were content with their lives except for their lack of a child. Finally their prayers were answered and a son was born to them. They named him Nicholas, which means "victorious."

Even in infancy Nicholas showed signs of being especially devout. It is said that on Wednesdays and Fridays, church fast days, he refused soft foods and his mother's milk except for once each day. During his first bath he stood right up in the basin and raised his hands over his head in an effort to praise the Lord.

As a young boy, Nicholas did not involve himself in the games and pranks of the other children of Patara but spent his time at church studying scripture. He then strived to live according to the Christian principles he had learned.

He was nine years old when a plague swept through his village. Both his father and mother died. Although Nicholas moved in with friends of his parents, he felt lost without the two people he had loved so dearly. Bereft of his parents, who was the orphan to love?

As Nicholas grew older he learned to share the love he had given his parents with the people of his village. His father had left him a small inheritance, which enabled him to give gifts of food, clothing, or money to the poor. Nicholas was careful to remain anonymous with his charities. Most of his gift giving was done at night when he could hide under the cover of darkness.

One day Nicholas learned that a friend of his father had fallen into poverty. His three daughters, like all maidens of that time, wanted to be happily married. Without money for a dowry, however, marriage was impossible. One of the girls decided to sell herself as a slave,

ensuring that at least her sisters could be properly wed.

Nicholas was horrified when he learned of this and decided to intervene. Late that night he made his way to their home, tossed a bag of gold through the window, then slipped away before he was discovered. Legend says the gold coins fell into a stocking that had been hung there to dry. Two more nights he crept to the window, each time throwing a bag of gold to the sleeping girls.

On the third night, the gold clattered to the floor and awakened the young girls' father. He pursued his unknown benefactor through the darkened streets. When he discovered it was Nicholas who had saved his daughter from a life of bondage, he knelt and attempted to kiss Nicholas' feet. Nicholas refused this homage and requested that the man keep the incident a secret. He agreed and only divulged the information on his deathbed.

As a result of this story, portraits of St. Nicholas often show three golden balls in his hand. Each ball represents a bag of gold tossed into the window.

Nicholas died December 6, around A.D. 343. The day was then set aside in honor of this man whose good works and deeds lived on in the hearts of the people he had served.

Nicholas traveled to the Holy Land to continue both his education and religious training while still in his teens. On the return voyage, the ship was overtaken by a violent storm and the frightened sailors pleaded with him to pray. He agreed and knelt on the deck as the storm tossed the ship for two days. When the storm decreased they made safe harbor at Myra, a town near his village of Patara.

Nicholas was unaware that the Bishop of Myra had died and that other bishops and church leaders were assembled to elect a new bishop for that district. The night before Nicholas' ship entered the harbor, one of

44

the bishops heard the voice of God during the night, instructing him to watch the doors of the church during the hour of matins or morning prayer. He was told that the next man named Nicholas to enter the church should become the new bishop.

Thankful that God had delivered his ship from the storm, Nicholas went directly to the chapel to pray. As he entered, the watchful bishop demanded his name. When he replied, "Nicholas," the man said to him, "Nicholas, servant and friend of God, for your holiness ye shall be bishop of this place."

Still a youth, Nicholas did not feel equal to the task. However, the bishop was convinced that God himself had chosen Nicholas and the devout young man's protests were swept aside.

Nicholas is credited with many miracles throughout his ministry as Bishop of Myra. One recorded story tells of a woman who rushed from her home upon hearing the new bishop was in town. In her excitement she left her baby waiting for his bath in a pot of water over the fire. When she remembered, the terrified mother beseeched Nicholas to save him. He sent her home with his blessing. There she found the baby unharmed and playing happily with the bubbles from the boiling water.

Years later, a great famine desolated the land. The people suffered from near starvation. When Nicholas was notified that several ships laden with wheat had entered the harbor at Myra, he approached their captains and asked them to donate a portion of their cargo to his famished people.

They replied, "Father we dare not, for it is meted and measured, and we must give reckoning thereof in the garners of the Emperor in Alexandria."

Nicholas answered, "Do this that I have said to you, and I promise, in the truth of God, that it shall not be lessened or diminished when you come to the garners."

The captains agreed and left wheat to feed the people for two years, as well as enough for the farmers to plant.

When the captains unloaded their cargo in Alexandria, they found a full shipment as promised.

Another legend tells of a ship grounded on rocks during a gale. Afraid the ship would sink and all aboard would perish in the turbulent sea, the sailors prayed to the distant Bishop Nicholas. As they prayed, Nicholas appeared flying toward them through the air. When he landed on the deck the storm abated. Nicholas prayed with the crew, helped them free the ship from the rocks, then flew away. (Perhaps this story gave our modern Santa Claus the ability to fly as he delivers his gifts.) When the ship arrived in the harbor at Myra, the sailors went directly to Nicholas' church and were amazed to find him standing in front of the altar.

Nicholas died December 6, around A.D. 343. The day was then set aside in honor of this man whose good works and deeds lived on in the hearts of the people he had served. People referred to him as a saint long before the church officially began to canonize early Christians.

Over the years St. Nicholas became the patron saint of Russia, parish clerks, and pawnbrokers. He was also adopted by sailors, fisherman, dockers, coopers, brewers, travelers, and pilgrims. He is probably best known as the patron saint of unmarried women and children.

The people of Myra buried him in a beautiful crypt within a church that became the first of hundreds to bear his name. In 1087 Italian sailors who visited the Church of St. Nicholas in Myra stole the saint's remains and carried them to Bari in Italy. For this reason he is sometimes known as St. Nicholas of Bari.

Stories of St. Nicholas spread throughout the world. His fame grew as years passed and his image slowly began to change.

45

Father Christmas evolved from Roman homage to the god Saturn and the tradition of celebrating his winter feast, Saturnalia.

In Holland, however, Protestant children continued to celebrate St. Nicholas Day on December 6. In 1624 when Dutch immigrants sailed to America, the celebration of St. Nicholas arrived with them. Their first church in the New World was named St. Nicholas and the ship they sailed in, the *Goedevrouw*, had a figurehead of St. Nicholas on its hull.

Stories of St. Nicholas spread throughout the world. His fame grew as years passed and his image slowly began to change.

The Dutch, however, were not the first to celebrate St. Nicholas Day in the New World. On the evening of December 6, 1492, Christopher Columbus arrived in the West Indies. In honor of the saint whom he had celebrated his entire life and whose feast day it was, Columbus named the harbor *Puerto de San Nicolas,* or Port of St. Nicholas. Later, around 1784, a Spanish fort was built on the south side of the St. Johns River in what is now Jacksonville, Florida. In honor of their revered saint, the Spanish soldiers named the fort *San Nicolas.*

In New Amsterdam, the first Dutch settlement, St. Nicholas shed his bishop's robes and dressed more like the men of the 1600s. His Dutch name was *Sinter Claes* or *Sancte Claus*. He wore a flat, broad-brimmed hat and smoked a long Dutch pipe. He also lost his tall, thin figure. Instead, *Sancte Claus* was short and chubby.

In 1664 Great Britain took control of New Amsterdam, and changed the name to New York. The English began to settle in the New World and brought their custom of Father Christmas, who delivered his gifts on Christmas Eve. The Dutch continued to believe in *Sinter Claes* or *Sancte Claus* and received gifts from him on December 6, St. Nicholas Day.

As the years passed, Dutch and English intermarried and Father Christmas and *Sancte Claus* blended into one figure. By the end of the American Revolutionary War, St. Nicholas, Bishop of Myra, was generally known in the United States as Santa Claus.

St. Nicholas, or Santa Claus, has another well-known counterpart. German immigrants brought to Pennsylvania the belief in their gift giver the *Christkindl,* or Christ child. As with the Dutch and English, intermarriage between the German and English produced a mingling of customs. Kriss Kringle emerged, resembling *Pelze Nichol* or fur clad Nicholas.

The first person to write about St. Nicholas in the newly formed United States was Washington Irving. A native of New York City, he wrote a satirical novel entitled *A History of New York from the Beginning of the New World to the End of the Dutch Dynasty.* The book was authored under the pseudonym of Diedrich Knickerbocker and was published on December 6, 1890—St. Nicholas Day in Old Amsterdam.

In this book, Irving describes St. Nicholas dressed in traditional Dutch garb. Black Pete, who had accompanied St. Nicholas in Holland, was not mentioned at all. Instead, Irving had St. Nicholas himself flying over rooftops and dropping presents down the chimneys.

In Holland, St. Nicholas retained his bishop's robes but acquired a white horse and helper. Black Peter was a devilish looking character with red eyes and horns on his head. It was Black Peter who slid down chimneys and, on the advice of the saint, delivered presents to the good children and birch rods to the bad.

In remembrance of St. Nicholas tossing the three bags of gold to the sleeping maidens, Dutch congregations filled three wooden shoes with money on December 5 and placed them on the church altars. The money was then distributed to the poor in St. Nicholas' name.

Dutch children placed empty wooden shoes next to their fireplaces on St. Nicholas Eve. This custom spread and by the late 1400s children all over Europe were putting out empty shoes or stockings on December 5.

In northern Germany, Nicholas lost his bishop's robes and became known as *Pelze Nichol,* or fur-clad Nicholas. As in Holland, German children set out shoes on December 5 and found candy and goodies in them the next morning. However, German children also placed notes in their shoes for St. Nicholas to deliver to *Christkindl,* the Christ child, who delivered gifts on Christmas Day.

Tradition says that a day was set aside to celebrate the birth of Christ as early as A.D. 98. It was considered a solemn feast day by Telesphorus, Bishop of Rome, A.D. 137. However, the specific date of December 25 as the day to commemorate the birth of Christ was not officially set until A.D. 350 by Julius I, Bishop of Rome.

In the mid 1500s, Protestant churches under the leadership of Martin Luther were being formed. Luther denounced the worship of saints, especially St. Nicholas. By the 1600s the day of gift giving had been changed in many countries to Christmas Day.

In England, after St. Nicholas Day was no longer observed, the role of gift giver fell to Father Christmas. He was a large man who wore scarlet robes lined with fur.

In 1822 a professor named Clement Moore, also a native of New York City, wrote a poem for his small children. He did more to influence our modern image of Santa Claus than any other person. In this poem Santa's physical characteristics, dress, and mode of travel were made graphic.

"A Visit from St. Nicholas" was written in December of 1822 and read by Moore to his family on Christmas Eve. A young woman who was present at the reading asked for a copy. The next Christmas she mailed it to the editor of a small New York state newspaper where it was printed anonymously for the first time December 23, 1823, in the *Troy Sentinel*.

A Dutch handyman who worked for Moore at his home, Chelsea House, in what is now midtown Manhattan, is thought to have been the model for Moore's Santa Claus. The transformation from the tall, thin, stately Bishop of Myra into a plump, jolly old man, became complete as Moore described St. Nicholas to his children.

> *He had a broad face and a round little belly*
> *That shook, when he laughed, like a bowl*
>   *full of jelly.*
> *He was chubby and plump—a right jolly old elf,*
> *And I laughed, when I saw him, in spite of myself.*

Why an elf? Perhaps Moore had friends from Sweden who had told him tales of their gift giver, *Jultomte*. *Jultomte* wore a red hat, had a long white beard, and was an elf. Or perhaps Moore could visualize an elf sliding down chimneys easier than a full-grown man.

Moore had undoubtedly read a booklet published anonymously in 1821. *A New Year's Present for the Little Ones from Five to Twelve* was the name of Volume III of *A Children's Friend*. It was all about Christmas, and for the first time Santa Claus was pictured driving a sleigh pulled by one single reindeer. In Moore's poem he not only increased the number of reindeer to eight, but gave them each a name. These reindeer have become, in the twentieth century, as famous as Santa Claus himself.

There is little doubt that Moore drew on the description in Washington Irving's novel. In one scene Irving has his St. Nicholas "laying a finger beside his nose" before climbing into his wagon and flying away. Surely that is where Moore got his notion of how St. Nicholas would climb back *up* the chimney after leaving the presents:

> *And laying his finger aside of his nose,*
> *And giving a nod, up the chimney he rose.*

Moore also dressed St. Nicholas in fur "from his head to his foot." This could have been taken from the German custom of celebrating *Pelze Nichol* or Nicholas dressed in fur.

Thomas Nast, a cartoonist for *Harper's Weekly Magazine,* is the next person credited with aiding the transformation of St. Nicholas, Bishop of Myra, to Santa Claus, jolly gift giver. Born in Germany in 1840, Nast immigrated to the United States with his family when he was eight years old. His first picture of Santa Claus, a pen and ink drawing, appeared in Harper's Weekly Magazine in 1863. For the next 23 years, until 1886, Nast drew a new Santa picture for this magazine each Christmas season. It was Nast who gave Santa Claus the North Pole

for an address and pictured him in his workshop surrounded by toys.

Besides giving Santa a home at the North Pole, Nast made another important contribution. When asked to reproduce seven of his close-up portraits into a book using the newly developed color printing, a decision had to be made. Until then, all portraits of Santa had been in black and white. Nast may have chosen red for Santa's suit simply because it is such a vibrant color even in

Thomas Nast, a cartoonist for *Harper's Weekly Magazine,* is credited with aiding the transformation of St. Nicholas, Bishop of Myra, to Santa Claus, jolly gift giver. It was Nast who gave Santa Claus the North Pole for an address and pictured him in his workshop surrounded by toys.

print, or he may have chosen this color in honor of the red bishop's robes that St. Nicholas himself wore.

In 1931 Haddon Sundblom was commissioned by Coca Cola to illustrate Christmas ads that depicted Santa Claus drinking this popular beverage. Basically the same jolly, robust character as in the Nast pictures, Sundblom made one important change. Santa was no longer an elf but a full-grown man nearly six feet tall. It is the Sundblom image that people today visualize when they hear the name Santa Claus.

Missionaries spread Christianity around the globe and introduced the celebration of Christmas into non-Christian cultures. In Africa, Dutch and English immigrants brought with them St. Nicholas and Father Christmas. In time these famous gift givers adapted to the hot and steamy climate of the jungle in December.

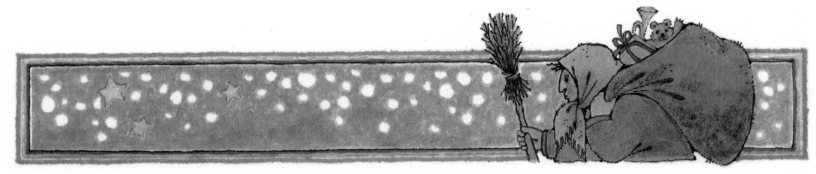

In Kenya, Santa Claus can be found wearing a safari suit or pictured in a bathing suit on the beach. Instead of a sleigh pulled by reindeer, he rides in a donkey cart pulled by impala, a type of native deer. In Ghana and the Union of South Africa, the English Father Christmas delivers gifts on Christmas Eve. His address is not the North Pole but the jungle.

In other mostly non-Christian countries St. Nicholas did not become part of the Christmas celebration. In Japan, for instance, *Hoteiosho* is a kindly old man who carries presents in a large pack on his back. He also has eyes in the back of his head in order to better watch the behavior of children throughout the year.

In China where approximately one percent of the over one billion people are Christian, the Chinese have their own gift givers. *Lan Khoong-Khoong*, Nice Old Father, or *Dun Che Lao Ren*, Christmas Old Man, puts gifts in stockings the children hang on Christmas Eve.

In parts of Europe and other Christian countries, St. Nicholas is known but not as gift giver. For instance, in Spain, Mexico, and other Spanish speaking countries, it is the Magi or three Wise Men who deliver gifts on the Eve of Epiphany, January 6. This is to commemorate the arrival of the Wise Men in Bethlehem where they presented gifts of gold, frankincense, and myrrh to the baby Jesus. Christmas remains a religious celebration and St. Nicholas merely a saint whose feast day falls during the Christmas season.

Italian children also receive gifts on Epiphany Eve, but from a woman. Legend says that an old woman named *Befana* was invited to accompany the three Wise Men to Bethlehem. She declined, saying she had too much housework to do. The next day she changed her mind and tried unsuccessfully to catch up with the Wise Men. To this day she vainly searches for the baby Jesus on Epiphany Eve. During her journey she fills the children's shoes with presents to make up for the gift she did not give the Christ child.

In Christian Russia another old woman delivers gifts on Epiphany Eve. When the Wise Men asked *Baboushka* which road led to Bethlehem, she purposely gave wrong directions. After they left, she regretted her deception, but it was too late to stop the Wise Men. For penance, she travels throughout Russia every Epiphany Eve and places gifts under the children's pillows, in hopes that the Christ child will be one of them.

Today in the Soviet Union, a nonreligious figure called Grandfather Frost delivers gifts to the Russian children on New Year's Eve. He is white-bearded, chubby, and dresses in red, fur-trimmed clothes, much like Santa Claus.

It is difficult to discern any physical trace of Nicholas, the actual Christian saint, in the character figure we have named Santa Claus. His modern appearance is a composite of three European Christmas figures that have come down to us: England's Father Christmas who delivers gifts on Christmas Eve rather than on St. Nicholas Eve, Holland's red-robed Bishop Nicholas who changed his attire in the New World to include a long Dutch pipe, and Germany's *Pelze Nichol*, or Nicholas dressed in fur.

The writings of Clement Moore not only transformed the tall, painfully thin Bishop Nicholas into a chubby elf, but the bishop's solemn face etched with lines of concern and responsibility also disappeared:

> *His eyes, how they twinkled! His dimples, how*
> *   merry!*
> *His cheeks were like roses, his nose like a cherry!*
> *His droll little mouth was drawn up like a bow,*
> *And the beard of his chin was as white as the snow.*

Yet Santa's selfless spirit does go back almost 1700 years to the saintly Nicholas, Bishop of Myra. The tradition of gift giving was born of his devotion to God—a devotion he demonstrated through a sincere and unpretentious life of service to his people. This spirit of giving has endured through the centuries and emerges again in our own Christmas season embodied in the folk hero we call Santa Claus.

Can You Gift-Wrap A Reflection?

LOIS RAND

WHISPERS, CRACKLING with excitement, come from behind a closed door. "Isn't it beautiful?" "Yeah, Mom will just love it!" "Let's wrap it right away and hide it where she can't find it." "I can't wait to give it to her! Oh, I love Christmas!" Giggles mix with the rustling of paper.

A variation on that theme is repeated in countless homes every December. Nothing is so much fun as planning a surprise for someone you love; and a gift is a tangible surprise that will last. We're willing to spend an incredible amount of time and money seeking those tangible surprises. It's part of the Christmas tradition, after all—gift-giving and gift-receiving.

Certainly the gifts aren't everything there is to Christmas. For all of us there is more. We know it's a holy season. We will worship, hearing the manger story and singing the carols with joy and nostalgia. We will greet family and friends with exuberant good wishes, and probably eat too much with them. And yes, we will give and receive those brightly colored packages that have preoccupied us for weeks. Mother will cherish and exclaim over that gift so lovingly wrapped and giggled over.

Sometimes, though, quite different scenes are part of the preparation and the day itself. Often nice, civilized—even Christian—people enact them. Listen!

Time is growing short. Mother checks her gift list and heads for the mall. She must buy something appropriate for each one listed, gift-wrap and often mail the packages. She also has to bake and finish the Christmas cards. She mutters, "I just dread Christmas. I'll never be ready in time."

It is two days before Christmas. Between phone calls, the busy executive instructs his secretary, "Pick up a gift for my wife on your lunch hour, will you? Something nice . . . you know her type. And have the store gift-wrap it. My schedule is too full to think about it."

The child pulls package after package out from beneath the tree. There is a flurry of paper-ripping and box-opening, discovering contents, playing with them momentarily or moving on to the next package at once. Mother may remind, "Say thank you to Uncle Bill," and this courtesy is dispatched with haste so as not to delay the action unduly. At last, the child scrabbles through the pile of paper and ribbon and says in a tone of disappointment, "Is that all?"

> God gave his gift to the undeserving, but many half-pagan practices grew out of less lofty and generous philosophies . . . resulting in the stunning use and abuse we call Christmas.

Frustration, frenzy, callousness, disappointment, and enormous excesses have somehow encroached on the holy day. They have become habits, bad habits muddled together with good ones.

"Christmas has become so commercialized," we say, and that is true. The avalanche of advertising beginning in late summer and the extravaganza of holiday merchandise on display seem to push us far from the heart and meaning of the first Christmas. Yet giving and generosity are hallmarks of God's great gift of his Son to us.

Imagine! God sent that gift to a world that was undeserving, not particularly interested, and unprepared to reciprocate. It was simply *given*—out of love and because we needed it. From this great act has grown the

concept of gift giving, resulting at last in the stunning collection of use and abuse we call Christmas.

How did this happen? How did the substance of Christmas come to be drowned in spectacle and commerce? Looking back through the centuries, we can see that nobody set out to spoil things. History is full of illuminating insights for anyone who wants to distinguish between celebrating Christmas truly and falsely.

Since long before the first Christmas, gifts have been used to express love, honor, and respect. We know that Jesus' birth prompted just such a response. The Magi not only worshiped and adored after their long trip, but presented gold, frankincense, and myrrh. We remind ourselves of this every time a Sunday school child in a bathrobe carries a fancy bottle of bath salts to an improvised manger. And it is worth remembering that VIPs from distant lands did bring their finest possessions to this humble baby. We wonder what his family may have done with them, but they were gifts of great love.

Pagan festivals of that time, such as the Roman Saturnalia in late December, included gift giving as part of the riotous celebrations. Early Christians discouraged such celebrating and attempted to exert an influence on their culture. They began to substitute the giving of less expensive gifts and to emphasize the spirit of love and generosity characteristic of the Christmas story.

The fourth century yields the first real clue, after the Magi, as to Christian gift customs. St. Nicholas, Bishop of Myra in Turkey, was a devout and compassionate man who believed fervently that his calling as a Christian was to help those in need. He often sought out persons in miserable straits, or poor children, and gave them money, tossing a bag of coins through a window in the dark of night. Some said he occasionally tossed the money down a chimney, where it might roll into a stocking or slipper by the hearth. After this beloved bishop died one December 6, gifts were often given on that date in his honor. The proximity of December 6 to the observation of Christmas, as well as the mutual message of generosity, forged a tie between the two.

The story of St. Nicholas seems to be the basis for many later Christmas gift customs. It was carried from Constantinople to Russia and finally to Europe's northern nomadic tribes. One wonders if at some point the Lapps added the reindeer and the sleigh.

Sometimes Christmas tales and legends mingled with pagan beliefs, with odd results. In all of them, however, gifts appear. The chimney and stocking version, suggested in the St. Nicholas account, appeared also in old Germanic tales. These claimed that *Erda,* goddess of the home, came down hidden in smoke and put goodies for children in a slipper on the hearth. Parents began using this as a handy device to entice children to be good, and from it was born a concept entirely contradictory to the Christian message. God gave his gift to the undeserving, but many half-pagan practices grew out of less generous and lofty philosophies.

St. Nicholas himself had been faithful to his conviction that gifts should be given anonymously to those in need, so that Christ alone would be honored. However, the incentive of being good so as to receive gifts persisted until at last in many European countries St. Nicholas was riding through the air on his horse, checking on children's behavior, and then bringing gifts to good children and switches or lumps of coal to bad ones. One shudders to think what this concept taught about the Christ child. (Martin Luther tried to counteract such distortion by saying that Jesus' messenger, *Christkindl,* later called Kriss Kringle, brought the gifts.)

It is interesting that although these national customs vary widely, they all have to do with receiving more than giving. The gifts come from some mysterious or supernatural source.

Another set of legends created an entirely different set of customs in some places. Russia and Italy developed practices apparently stemming from a common origin. Russian children believed that an old crone named *Baboushka* had misdirected the Magi on their search for the Christ child, and had also refused to help the holy family on their flight into Egypt. Her punishment was to journey through the countryside every Christmas Eve, searching the homes for the baby Jesus. Whenever she found a sleeping child, she slipped gifts under its pillow. Italian children cherished the same story, called the woman *La Befana,* and hung their clothes out where she could fill the pockets with candy and toys.

The countries along the Mediterranean also developed the practice of gift-giving at Epiphany, the Feast of the Magi, on January 6. Children would leave straw for the Magi's camels and find it replaced by gifts in the morning.

Scandinavians showed no signs of expecting St. Nicholas, or the Magi, or any wandering crone as the gift-bringer. They relied on *Jultomte* or *Julenisse*, the Christmas elf, who rode, if he rode anything, a Christmas goat. He brought gifts but also expected to be treated well with a special Christmas repast. Failing that, he was considered able to make great trouble throughout the year. Charming as he is, his approach does introduce the idea of a swap: gifts for certain other considerations.

It is interesting that although these national customs vary widely as to the characters involved, the time of arrival, and mode of transportation, they all have to do with *receiving* more than *giving*. The gifts come from some mysterious or supernatural source. This at least hints at the original gift from God. Their chief emphasis is on children, perhaps because of the baby at the center of the original story, although he was not sent just to children. The gifts in many legends were candy, cookies, figgy pudding, sugar plums, oranges, nuts, and raisins—gifts of a simpler time.

The idea of need as a factor was largely lost. One should note, though, the British custom of Boxing Day, December 26. Originally, those in poor circumstances solicited from the more fortunate and carried boxes to collect the results. More recently, British countries have regarded Boxing Day as a time to bring gifts to servants, tenants, tradespeople, and certain dependents, or even simply to make calls on friends. It is one of the few historic examples of specific adult Christmas giving.

So as you and I make our lists, gather and wrap, and give to those we wish to remember we're no doubt doing so out of a tangle of customs, habits, and expectations that have spanned centuries. They may have strayed far from the spirit of God's Christmas gift to us, or even of the Magi's in return. It would be good to look harder at that first Christmas gift, and good also to consider our own gift habits in relation to it.

What should we ask ourselves? Are the things we are giving true Christmas gifts, or are they something else? A true Christmas gift, that is, one that is different from a gift given for some other occasion, should reflect what Christmas teaches about gifts. The first gift was later described: "The gift of God is eternal life in Jesus Christ our Lord" (Romans 6:23). That gift is the model for us. Nothing we give to or receive from others can be even a faint imitation of such lavishness. But the nature of the giving can be emulated.

The dictionary defines a gift as something given voluntarily without charge. From this, we can also easily see what a gift is *not*. It is not a reward for good behavior, and all those department store Santas who ask, "Have you been good?" before they make their promises are doing us mischief. A gift is not a human incentive plan. A gift is not an empty gesture, given as a formality or because it is expected. A gift is not an atonement for failure. A gift is not a way to purchase love or favor. A gift is not valued by quantity or cost. All these views point away from a true Christmas gift, but most of us would have to confess that such characteristics are often part of our gift-giving.

> All those department store Santas who ask, "Have you been good?" before they make their promises are doing us mischief. A gift is not a human incentive plan.

In centuries to come, what will the legends and customs of our time say about us Christians and our convictions? In fact, what do they say now? The late journalist, Sydney Harris, once commented about the over-commercialization of Christmas: "It is not the impious and unbelievers who must be on guard . . . it is the believers. . . . It is easy to think Christmas and to believe Christmas, but it is hard—sometimes very hard—to act Christmas."

To act Christmas—what a lofty goal! Can our gift-giving say something true, reflect something real? Can we take charge of this unruly set of traditions to which we are heir and improve them? Before assembling a gift list, could we assemble a checklist of standards by which to measure our gift decisions? Such a list might go like this:

Adoration of the Christ child comes first. Those who have little or no means to devote to human giving can give hearts full of thanks to God and can share the gift of this thanksgiving with others. But most of us face another problem. We may need to remind ourselves to concentrate on adoration rather than on the plenty out

of which we are accustomed to celebrate. Adoration sheds the brightest of reflections.

Give as unto the Christ child. First on our gift list will be those in need, those who can never reciprocate. Jesus said, "Inasmuch as you did it to one of the least of these, you did it to me" (Matthew 25:40). This may mean less "exchanging" among associates, less lavish quantities poured upon loved ones, more attention to "the least of these." To accomplish this may mean spending more time praying and preparing the heart than shopping and preparing the packages. But how brightly such a guideline will reflect the Father's gift and honor the manger baby!

Give from a loving heart. Kind thoughts will put their stamp on every package wrapped for others. No grudging reluctance, no mechanical repetition will tarnish the reflection of such gifts. As Luther said, "The heart of the giver makes the gift dear and precious."

Give without expecting a return. After all, favors given with reciprocal expectations are not gifts but trades. We have already received our precious gift; all the others should flow from that. A reflection of God's gift is a selfless one.

Give something of yourself in every gift. Tasha Tudor, in her book, *Take Joy*, recounts the beautiful old legend of the raven bringing the news of Jesus' birth to the other birds. Quickly the birds responded in their individual ways. The wren wove a blanket of feathers, leaves, and moss for the baby. The rooster announced the birth from the housetops, crowing, *"Christus natus est."* The nightingale sang the baby a lullaby. And the robin shielded him from the fierce heat of the open fire.

We can make our giving that personal, too. We can spend time making a gift or give careful thought to selecting something that will show we love and understand the recipient. Two great writers have urged this point. James Russell Lowell emphasized that "the gift without the giver is bare," and Kahlil Gibran reminded, "You give but little when you give your possessions. It is when you give of yourself that you truly give." Giving of self will reflect the gift Jesus made of himself to the world.

Ask yourself and your friends for memories of special gifts from Christmases past. The most vivid memories are usually not of gifts given or received, but of the spirit of love, the special warmth of Christmas worship, the cherished little habits of the home, the results of others acting in the spirit of Christ. Even memories of gifts are usually precious for something other than glamour or monetary value: a first shaving kit for an adolescent boy, a handmade book of coupons offering youthful assistance to a weary mother, even, as one woman recalled from her childhood, a new baby sister for an only child. As different as these gifts are, their common denominator and the reason they are remembered, is that they touched each individual so personally with a sense of being loved and cherished.

We can go with the tide, overspending and underthinking ourselves into exhaustion and disillusion until Christmas seems empty or forbidding or, perhaps, deceptively glorious.

Ours is a society awash in a materialism perhaps most evident in the Christmas season. We can go with the tide, overspending and underthinking ourselves into exhaustion and disillusion until Christmas seems either empty or forbidding or, perhaps, deceptively glorious for the wonder of what we have done. Or we can dig in our heels and rebel against the whole process as a corruption. Neither extreme will say what a Christian wants to say about Christmas.

Wiser, perhaps, is to realize that the heart of the matter is how we think and feel about *real* Christmas. What is our attitude, first toward the Lord's gift to us, and then toward those with whom we observe and honor that gift? The challenge is to find a way to be true to the spirit of the first Christmas, then to seek ways to reflect its wonderful meaning in our planning and shopping *and* under our Christmas trees.

Christmas generosity as a custom is nothing special, but as an attitude it is significant. Gifts to the needy, under the tree, or anywhere else will cast reflections. "Be sure Jesus shows" is not just good advice when we set up our nativity scenes, but in all our preparing and celebrating.

Listen! Pray that we do not hear, "I just dread Christmas. . . . My schedule is too full to think about it. . . . Is that all there is?" Listen instead for "I love Christmas," reflecting lives that love because God loves, give because God gives, and never forget to let Jesus show.

Christmas Corners

Christmas Forever

CEIL McLEOD

AT 4:30 P.M. ON CHRISTMAS EVE, I finished placing gifts around our poor excuse for a Christmas tree with its saggy felt ornaments. The tree, a two foot potted Norfolk pine, stood on a candle stand in a corner of our living room.

I sighed. Months of concern over the break-up of our son Hugh's ten-year marriage had smothered my Christmas spirit. Even the addition of miniature Swedish horses circled by red candles in tiny china pots did little to help the tree.

Maybe I should have listened to my husband when he suggested picking up a large Douglas fir tree. But this year it seemed to me a waste of money, for no Christmas bells rang in my heart.

As I sat back, comparing prior Christmases with rocking horses and dolls, this year's practical gifts of shirts, sweaters, and books seemed dull. Yesterday's toys seemed as far away as yesterday's dreams of happy marriage for our children.

The thought hit me. Does a person have to have children around to display a toy or two? If the sight of a doll would lift my heart, why not?

Before I could change my mind, I dashed to the guest room bureau, opened the bottom drawer, and peeled back tissue from around the china-headed doll of my childhood, Mary. I'd forgotten the sweetness of her smile, her brown lashes edging closed eyes.

I smoothed her long organdy dress, carried her tenderly to the tree, and propped her at the base with her arms raised expectantly. Then I sank into a velvet-covered rocker. Time stopped as I rocked and gazed at the doll.

The sound of the doorbell startled me. It must be Hugh, who had called earlier to ask if he could bring a friend to dinner. Before I could reach the door, a slender girl with warm brown eyes entered, followed by Hugh.

He hugged me, then taking her hand he announced, "Mom, this is Linda." I noted with joy that some of the old bounce was back in his voice.

Her handshake was firm, her smile friendly. While Hugh arranged his gifts around the tree, Linda was drawn to the doll. With her finger, she traced the doll's cheek. "She's beautiful. May I hold her?" she asked.

"Of course, why don't you sit here in the rocker?" I answered.

She slipped into the chair and cuddled the doll in her arms while our son sprawled on the floor gazing at her, a smile on his lips.

I enjoyed the scene from my nearby wing chair.

> **Months of concern over the breakup of our son Hugh's ten-year marriage had smothered my Christmas spirit.**

"Where did you get her?" Linda asked, winding a strand of the doll's brown hair around her finger.

"She was under the tree the Christmas when I was seven. It was a Christmas I'll never forget," I paused.

"Please tell us about it," Linda begged. Hugh took his eyes from her long enough to grin at me.

"All right, but stop me if you get bored."

"Don't worry, mother," he said.

It was Christmas of 1923. I woke up that morning with only one thought in mind. Was there a china-headed doll under the tree for me? Two years earlier I'd fallen in love with a china doll with cropped brown hair, propped up in Fairchild's department store window. When I begged for her, my parents said, "No, dear, she's too expensive and fragile for a little girl." But I never gave up hoping.

That morning, together with my brothers, Bill and Steve, I raced through my oatmeal. For once, washed down with gulps of milk, it didn't gag me. Bowls clean, we leaned against the mahogany sliding doors to the living room. It seemed hours before father called, "Come in!"

The doors slid open, revealing a tree glittering with lights in shiny holders. Tinsel sparkled. Halfway across the room I sniffed the piney fragrance. I stood motionless, gazing from the silver star on top to branches decked with icicles, garlands of gold, and hand-painted Bohemian ornaments. Surely never before had there been such a tree.

My gaze fell to stacks of tissue-wrapped gifts tied with red silk ribbon at the tree's base. I knelt, searching for something soft and round like. . . . Nothing. My heart fell. Then I saw it. A tiny blue shoe peeked out from behind a tall package. Breathless I tugged the box aside. There, smiling, sat the very doll of my dreams, the doll I thought of as Mary. I swooped her into my arms. Under a ruffled bonnet, the doll's brown eyes seemed to smile at me.

"You've come, my very own china-headed baby." I hugged the doll and rocked her, oblivious of everyone.

Finally I looked up to see tears in mother's eyes. Even Steve had stopped winding his train to stare.

"Mary doll's finally come," I whispered. They smiled back.

"Ceil, read what the tag says on that tall package beside your knee," mother suggested.

"For Ceil," I read. "I made these clothes with love, dear. Your Aunt Mary."

"How did she know?" I wondered. Mother only smiled.

"Come, open it, dear," she said.

I couldn't bear to put Mary down even to open the package. Steve understood. "I'll help," he said, tearing away the tissue, revealing a sturdy doll wardrobe trunk with a brass catch. He spread the trunk open.

Wonder of wonders, it had three drawers on one side, a hat box and clothes on hangers on the other. I tried to swallow. It was almost too much to believe. Never had I seen such wonders: first a green velvet-lined cape with brown fur buttons, a ruffled pink organdy dress embroidered with blue flowers and ribbon streamers, a romper suit with lace collar and cuffs, smocked gingham dress with puff sleeves, shoes of black kid with miniature silver buckles, cambric slips, and, last of all, a bonnet of green taffeta trimmed with shiny red cherries and green velvet leaves.

A tiny blue shoe peeked out from behind a tall package. Breathless, I tugged the box aside. There, smiling, sat the very doll of my dreams.

Such oohing and aahing as I tried each outfit on the chubby baby figure. The day faded into evening. All day long I played with Mary and her lovely clothes. Finally, worn out, I climbed into the wing chair, my eyes heavy. Such a Christmas. I fell asleep hugging Mary.

Unknown to me, mother tip-toed in and felt my hot forehead. For safekeeping she placed Mary in a box with her trunk far back in the hall closet. Then she called our family doctor.

The news was grim, a bad case of whooping cough. My brothers were to stay away. Two days later, a pink rash appeared. The doctor checked me carefully, then shook his head. "This is serious," he said. "Ceil not only has whooping cough, but scarlet fever as well. She's a very sick little girl. Under quarantine law her brothers and father must move out or be confined to this apartment until the quarantine is lifted."

I remember little of those days except times when I pounded on the wall, trying to catch my breath, then fell back exhausted. That is until the night when I wakened in the dim light of a single hanging bulb to see mother leaning over my bed weeping. On the other side, the doctor held my wrist.

I felt like I was burning up. I heard mother's voice in a sort of haze. "Dear Lord, she's your child. You know what's best for her. But, oh, please spare her. Please let her live."

I seemed to be falling into a bright light. My breath came easier. I opened my eyes, surprised to see mother's face still wet with tears. I reached for her hand. "Don't cry, mother. It's Christmas," I said.

The doctor's deep voice surprised me. "Praise God, her fever's breaking. The crisis is over. Your prayer is answered."

Mother kissed me. "Thank you, Lord," she whispered. I smiled and fell into a deep sleep.

Later I found that two weeks had passed since Christmas while I'd lain desperately ill. I grew stronger. Gifts arrived: soft animals, boy and girl dolls in a straw box from Japan, a clown that jumped and climbed a ladder, and books with wonderful pictures. Mother put off my requests for Mary, saying I had enough with the new gifts.

One day mother wrapped me in a blanket and carried me to a window to wave at my brothers and father on

the ground below our apartment. As I grew stronger, I longed to run around. But the doctor ordered me to stay quiet to rest my heart, which was damaged by the illness.

A week later, mother began stripping down curtains and washing walls. She carried me to the living room couch, giving me old books to read. I heard shouts from the backyard.

"Mother, what's happening?" I called. No answer came.

Curious, I tip-toed to the back window, amazed to see flames leaping from a bonfire with neighbors gathered around. As I watched, mother tossed a leather ottoman onto the fire, then books. A pillow flamed up. I stared, bewildered. What were they doing? I watched in horror as my fuzzy lion caught fire, next the straw box, then something wrapped in a baby blanket. Could it be Mary? Could they be burning Mary?

"Stop it. Stop it!" I screamed, beating on the window.

Mother glanced up, then ran to the back door.

"They're burning Mary!" I screamed. That's all I remember until I felt mother tuck me into bed, feel my forehead. She kissed me. But I couldn't stop crying.

"Ceil, you'll bring your fever back," she admonished.

"I don't care," I sobbed even harder.

"Let me explain about the bonfire," mother said. I buried my head in the pillow. "If you'll stop crying, I'll tell you some good news." Mother's voice was firm. I lifted a corner of the pillow. "Mary's all right. Mary's all right."

I heard mother's voice in a kind of a daze. "Dear Lord, she's your child. You know what's best for her. But, oh, please spare her. Please let her live."

I opened my eyes, almost afraid to hear more. "You didn't burn Mary?" I asked between sniffs.

"No. You see, dear, by quarantine law we had to burn all your things so no one else would catch scarlet fever germs. However, before you came down with scarlet fever, I had placed your Mary doll in the hall closet. So she's safe. If you'll stay quiet, I'll bring her to you."

Propped up on pillows, I watched the door. In seconds she returned with Mary, and handed her to me. I hugged her as though she would fly away, her plaster body pressed against my chest.

"Ceil, there's more good news," mother continued. "Your period of quarantine is over. Tonight your father and brothers move back home."

"It seems like Christmas, mother!" I exclaimed.

"Yes, it does to me, too," mother answered. "And why not? Christmas is a time of the heart, not just a date. Jesus was born to love us and fill our lives with himself. He knew you needed Mary to love, and now he's made you well again and is bringing us all back together as a family. It *is* Christmas!"

As I finished the story, I noticed Linda's thoughtful look, while Hugh leaned forward, his blue eyes serious. "I don't ever remember hearing that story before," he said.

"I'd almost forgotten it myself until I placed Mary under the tree," I replied.

"Hi, everybody!" My husband, Hugh Sr., entered the room.

After introducing Linda, our son said, "You missed mom's story, dad."

"I'm sorry about that. I just finished a long distance call." He glanced from the doll in Linda's lap back to me and raised one eyebrow as though in question. His fingers squeezed mine.

At his touch memories flashed across my mind of God's answers to prayer over the years. Silently I thanked God for restoring my health years ago and for new beginnings following our son's divorce.

Restoring joy in family relationships has always been God's priority business, I thought. How wonderful it is that God's love breaks through hurt to rebuild lives and relight Christmas in our hearts.

Winter Activities of
A DAY GONE BY

PAINTINGS BY WILLIAM MEDCALF
TEXT BY JENNIFER HUBER

JINGLE BELLS! JINGLE BELLS!" Voices ring out, merrily singing this yuletide favorite: "Dashing through the snow in a one-horse open sleigh. . . !" Immediately our hearts brighten with Christmas cheer and thoughts of Christmases past flood our memories. Taking a closer look, however, we discover that the song says nothing at all about Christmas. It really is a "sleighing song." Why then do we associate "Jingle Bells" with Christmas? No doubt it's because Christmas has become a time for nostalgia, a time for looking back with fondness on the way things used to be. So we sing about an "open sleigh" even though few of us have ever seen one, much less dashed through the snow in one to grandmother's house on Christmas Day.

LONG THE CENTERPIECE of an elaborate Christmas Day
dinner, roast goose or turkey is an American holiday tradition.
Stuffed early Christmas morning with dressing made from mother's
"special recipe," it emerges from the oven hours later all shiny and
steamy in basted perfection. The family is called from the various corners
of the house to gather around the table. Heads bow in prayer. Then
comes the moment for the head of the house to carve the succulent bird.
Mouths water as plates are passed to receive a portion of this delicacy.

Nowadays, shoppers simply select their holiday goose or turkey from
the display at the meat counter or even from the frozen food section of
their local grocery store. In previous years, however, farm families raised
their own poultry. The fowl yard was an important part of the farmstead,
providing both eggs and meat for the farm family. Besides the ever-
present chickens (both hens and at least one rooster), the yard might
have contained a variety of ducks, geese, and turkeys.

During summer, the fowl would roam freely, feeding on seeds and
small insects. Come winter, however, the birds would be penned and fed
cracked corn to fatten them up. This not only helped to keep them warm
but also made for good eating around Thanksgiving and Christmas. Then
the prize turkey and the fattened goose would be singled out for the
family feast. Unlike the fryer chickens, the laying hens were locked in a
coop, where they tended to lay more eggs. A supply of fresh eggs was
needed, especially at Christmastime in order to prepare holiday recipes.

THE PEOPLE OF SCANDINAVIA have developed a charming holiday custom of feeding the birds on Christmas Day. A sheaf of wheat is set out on a pole from which the birds may eat. Because the northern climes tend to be harsh in winter, this act of charity can be a lifesaver to the little creatures.

For the cattle rancher, however, the provision of feed was not a one-time act of charity, but a daily chore. During the winter months not a day would go by that a cattle rancher didn't feed the herd, for without their daily ration of hay the cattle would quickly perish.

So it was important that sufficient hay be cut during the summer months and laid up for winter. When the grass had grown high in summer, the rancher would mow it and leave it to dry in the sun. Later the rancher would come back and collect the hay, piling it in mounds 10 to 15 feet high. Because the mounds sat directly on the ground, out in the elements, it was important to locate them in a place with adequate drainage. If piled in a low spot, the hay would act like a wick and draw up any standing rainwater.

When winter arrived and covered the grasslands with snow, a portion of the haystack would be sliced off, using a long serrated hay knife, then loaded onto a wagon and taken to the cattle. There the hay would be spread around on the ground. By the time the cattle finished eating, as well as any number of marauding elk, there would be nothing left over. And so the cattle would survive until the grasses grew green again.

BEFORE THE DAYS OF MODERN refrigeration, people relied on the ice formed by nature to cool their milk and keep other perishable foods fresh. Every larger town of 500 to 1000 people had its own icehouse where blocks of ice cut from the frozen lakes and rivers of winter were packed away for the warmer months. In the spring and summer, the iceman would deliver these blocks to the townspeople's homes, where they would be placed in wooden ice chests. Shortly after Christmas and New Year's, when the ice on the lakes and rivers had frozen to a depth of 1½ feet or more, the ice harvest crew would work long hours laying up enough ice for the summer months.

Cutting the ice into 1½- to 2-feet squares required specialized equipment, beginning with a horsedrawn rig fitted with a sharp blade. This blade was pulled along the surface of the ice, cutting a groove about eight inches deep. Next, using crowbars and special ice saws, the workers cut the scored ice into smaller, more manageable pieces. Then the blocks were lifted out of the water with an ice tongs and slid along a wooden platform onto a wagon. Once the wagon was full, it was pulled into town to the icehouse. There the ice was unloaded block by block and stacked inside, a layer of sawdust sprinkled between the blocks to help insulate them. Higher and higher the layers of ice would reach, until finally the shed was full. Shutting the doors behind them, the workers would breathe a sigh of relief, stretch their tired muscles, and think of winter's end.

LOGS CRACKLING ON THE HEARTH, the mantle strung with boughs of evergreen and brightly colored stockings, a tree gayly decorated shining from the corner—need we look any farther for the perfect Christmas setting? Easily the focal point of our Christmas scene, the fireplace was once the center of the home. Before the days of electricity and natural gas, wood provided heat for warmth and cooking.

Since it was vital that the woodpile be well-stocked year around, the task of chopping down trees and cutting them into firewood might continue all winter long. The sturdy workhorse could be counted on to pull heavy loads, even through deep snow and along icy roads. With the approach of winter, wagon wheels were replaced with runners, which would slide easily over the ice and snow. The runners also provided their own type of winter fun; boys especially loved to ride on the runners as the sled glided along, even though an occasional bump or lurch might send them flying into a snowbank.

One trip into the woods was eagerly awaited by the children when, just before Christmas, they bundled up to go in search for the best-looking evergreen tree around. It had to stand straight and be nicely rounded (although a gap here or there could be fixed with a hole drilled in the trunk and an extra branch neatly inserted). Then when the tree was covered with strings of popcorn and cranberries and sprinkled with tinsel and twinkling candles, without fail the family would step back and exclaim, "Oh, this is the most beautiful tree we've ever had!"

Christmas Summons The Child

ELIZABETH ST. JACQUES

CHRISTMAS. The sound of the word is absolutely creamy. Say it to the accompaniment of a carol and an angel whispers in my ear, making me melt like a marshmallow.

You'd think the mother of two adult sons would have long outgrown visions of sugarplums dancing in her head, but I haven't. Perhaps it's a necessary reprieve from the troubles of the world that when Christmas calls, the child in me leaps free. Whatever the reason, I've learned not to resist, because Christmas wins every time.

There is one condition necessary for a perfect Christmas, however: this Canadian must have snow. Having lived in northern Ontario all my life, it's unthinkable to imagine Christmas without it.

No doubt memory deceives. But when I was growing up it always seemed to snow on Christmas Eve, starting just before suppertime when darkness slipped in over our little town. As a child, it was a test of patience to finish the meal without sacrificing good manners so that one could rush out into the cold to welcome Christmas.

Every child knew that Christmas really began outdoors where fat fluffy flakes tumbled down through the wide amber beams of light given off by the streetlamps. Out there, you could feel Christmas touch your face, linger on your eyelashes, talk with a crunchy voice beneath your feet. In those days it was safe to taste Christmas on your tongue, but pollution makes it no longer wise or desirable.

Desirable still, although discouraged at my age, is the longing to leave "angel prints" in the snow. This is an art belonging to children only because they do it best: one hurls herself backwards into the freshly fallen snow and moves arms and legs back and forth to resemble an angel with wings and a wide full skirt. The trick is to leave no bootprints at the bottom—dead giveaways that a person, not an angel, made the print. So it is important to brush away any incriminating evidence, especially on Christmas Eve, because that's when honest-to-goodness angels swoop down during the night to grade each print. Heaven forbid if you should offend an angel!

There aren't many "angel prints" around anymore. Have children become disinterested or are they simply unaware? Perhaps "angel printing" has become a lost art.

In our home, the night the tree was decorated was almost as important as Christmas itself. It escapes me how the tall evergreen got into our living room. But one day it would be there, standing fluffy and green and smelling deliciously sweet of red pine.

Carols played on our wind-up Victrola while my big brothers and I strung colored lights and hung the various glass ornaments collected over the years. Mother was busy in the kitchen whipping up a secret recipe of Lux soap flakes and other mysterious ingredients which transformed into a thick white wonderfully scented "snow." This "snow," when plopped in big mounds on the tree's branches and allowed to harden, looked like the real thing. Our tree was the envy of the neighborhood and, as I recall, I made *sure* it was envied as I bragged liberally to my friends. I never did ask mother for the recipe, unfortunately—another lost art.

Christmas Eve found our family gathered around the old Lindsay player piano, belting out carols that must have made the angels cover their ears. But perhaps they returned at intervals to sniff mother's cinnamon cookies baking in the oven and the freshly popped corn that swam in real butter. Um-um, good!

When older, Christmas Eve included the honor of singing in the choir during midnight mass. My stomach buzzed with butterflies that bumped into each other while I sang my solos to a packed church. But I don't recall embarrassing myself or my family. Of course, not all memories are to be trusted.

After mass our family huddled together and scurried home in the nose-pinching cold to feast on hot meat pies mother had left warming in the oven and mugs of hot chocolate that chased away the chill.

Desirable still, though discouraged at my age, is the longing to leave "angel prints" in the snow.

Even in those early morning hours our home seemed to be filled with music and laughter, which I never wanted to end. But end it must have, because memories return of my being dragged out of bed next morning by the wonderful aroma of turkey roasting in the oven. Racing downstairs to the living room, the smell of pine took over, seeming stronger than ever and the lights on the tree so much brighter. Christmas morning always sharpens the senses.

I've tried not to make gift-giving an important part of Christmas, but it is all the same. Somehow even one little gift makes Christmas special. Certain gifts received during childhood remain close to the heart—like my first book (*Just Mary Stories*), which I carried everywhere and memorized by heart, and the black patent leather shoes which had stood in the Hudson's Bay window (which had my nose-prints all over it), and the delicate white collar that mother crocheted just for me.

The Christmas I was 14, great sobs of joy bounced from our living-room walls; my brother had given me the red silk dress covered in black lace that I'd made love to for months in the Eaton's catalog. Another Christmas, the red melton bomber jacket with the Montreal Canadiens team crest on the front, which was too, too expensive to dream about, became a reality through my parents. I wailed like a wounded lamb that time. What joy! So many gifts of love still cherished in memory.

Christmas Day brought relatives to our house by the droves. Grandfather, who shared his birthday with Jesus, was my very favorite. When he would bring out the violin that he had made and start to play those wonderful French-Canadian jigs and reels, mother was driven into a spirited step-dance that set the lampshades wobbling and the wooden floor vibrating. My uncle, who had swiped mother's silver teaspoons from the dining-room table, would play the spoons on his knee while my Dad joined in with his tiny marine band mouth organ. The rest of us clapped wildly and toe-tapped in our chairs. Everyone was working up an appetite for the meal, of course, laughing so hard our stomachs ached.

After awhile, we children slipped away to the musty basement where *two cases* of soda pop were stashed es-

pecially for us, and we'd treat ourselves to whichever flavor we wanted. My favorite was cream soda. (Once it was orange crush until I found a bug in the bottom of the bottle.) And there were Japanese oranges and mother's Swedish tea-ring cookies with cherries on top! No one dared touch the apple and cherry pies or the homemade preserves, though, until they were set on the upstairs table—not if she wanted to live. Even Christmastime had rules in our house.

Mealtime finally arrived with enough food to feed the town. Turkey and stuffing and cranberry sauce, plus French-Canadian dishes from mother's side of the family and Polish dishes from dad's, overflowed the table, followed by desserts of every kind.

The years slipped by, however, and suddenly I was living in a city far away from family. With a husband and two young sons of my own, I now experienced firsthand how much work went into Christmas and how much pleasure accompanied it.

We too played carols while decorating the tree. But because those were lean years for us and buying a tree from a lot was too expensive, it was my husband's job to drive out to the woods to find a tree each year. Oftentimes he returned with a pitifully malnourished specimen that had me in tears. So back he would go, only to return with an armful of green branches, which he would insert into holes drilled in the already standing skeleton. My husband, you see, comes from the waste-not, want-not era. Each time, tears turned into laughter. We couldn't help *but* laugh: surely we had the most original Christmas tree anywhere!

Our Christmas Eves found us around our own piano now, singing the same lovely carols while my husband supplied backup music on his harmonica. Mother's Swedish tea-ring cookies appeared on our Christmas table the next day along with my mother-in-law's deep apple pie with the French topping.

As our sons grew older there were Christmases filled with young men and women playing the piano, one son on guitar, the other playing the flute. Always, always there was music and laughter and friendship.

OUR SONS are grown now and some Christmases they've been unable to join us. But as long as the memories remain, Christmas lives in the heart. And new memories are born, like the Christmas Eve my husband and I were returning home from visiting relatives now living in our city.

It was nearing midnight as we walked slowly home. The snow was falling softly, the world was as quiet as a breath. Stopping at the top of the hill, we said not a word as we stood looking out over the city awash in new white and flickering colored lights. Suddenly church bells began to peel, filling the night with beautiful, beautiful notes that rode on the air. I was a child again, bursting at the seams with Christmas, and I needed to do *something* to celebrate.

That night, a big smooth snowbank was stamped with two fully grown (although somewhat poorly executed) "angel prints." Both had telltale signs of bootprints at the bottom, so perhaps we offended the angels in our old age. Then again, maybe not. I like to think that angels understand the power of Christmas and how it has the ability to call out the child in each and every one of us.

Our Christmas

Christmas Eve _____
_____
_____
_____

Christmas Day _____
_____
_____

Christmas Worship _____
_____
_____
_____

Christmas Guests

_____
_____
_____
_____
_____
_____

Christmas Photo

Christmas Gifts

_____
_____
_____
_____
_____
_____